To my father,
the rock of my heritage and faith.

THE
FIVE MAJOR PIECES
TO THE
LIFE PUZZLE

by
E. JAMES ROHN

Printed by
Dickinson Press Inc.

Distributed by:
Jim Rohn International
2835 Exchange Blvd.
Suite 200
Southlake, TX. 76092
800-929-0434
www.jimrohn.com

Sign-up for
FREE weekly e-zine

info@jimrohn.com

Retail $12
ISBN 978-0-939490-02-8

TABLE OF CONTENTS

FOREWORD

It is the inherent nature of success to be both puzzling and elusive, and to withhold its rewards from all but a handful of those who pursue it.

It is by an intricate design of nature that success is a condition that must be attracted and not pursued. We achieve rewards and we make progress not by our intense pursuits, but by what we become, for it is what we are that finally determines the results we attract.

"To **have** more we must first **become** more" is the very essence of the philosophy of personal development, success and happiness addressed by Jim Rohn in The Five Major Pieces to the Life Puzzle.

It is our personal **philosophy** that establishes our individual attitude. It is our **attitude** that determines both the quantity and the quality of our level of activity. That activity produces a final and proportionate result, and the result provides the **lifestyle** that we live.

The results and the lifestyle are the effects — the conditions we inherit — but it is our personal philosophy, attitude and activity which are the ultimate cause of the effect.

To change the effect, we must alter the cause, and yet most people curse the effect but continue to nourish the cause.

In this, his third book, Jim Rohn brings ideas and insights in his inimitable style that provide a unique voice of hope, inspiration and answers for those in search of a better life. In the writing, he provides substance and encouragement to all those who embrace the philosophy of "You can have more than you've got because you can **become** more than you are."

Let the words touch you. Let the message of Jim Rohn inspire you. Allow Jim's philosophy to affect your life. After having read and mastered **The Five Major Pieces to the Life Puzzle,** you may well discover your potential as you have never before seen it!

Kyle Wilson
President
Jim Rohn International

THE
FIVE MAJOR PIECES
TO THE
LIFE PUZZLE

INTRODUCTION

At this moment in time you hold in your hands a document that represents an awesome force, and I trust that you will be as serious about *reading* this book as I have been about writing it.

What your eyes are now scanning are merely words on a printed page. The words and the thoughts they convey have a unique power. Our objective – yours and mine – will be to transform these printed words into ideas and emotions that will become the tools with which to fashion a new life, with new goals, and with a new resolve for attaining whatever you want to have and becoming whatever you wish to be.

Most books are written to entertain or inform. *This* book is written so that it might *inspire*. By virtue of the fact that you have come into possession of this book, there is the strong suggestion that you are already in the process of looking for something. There is also a strong possibility that there is something in your life you would like to change. Perhaps you feel that you are worth more than you are currently being paid or that you have more talent and ability than your current occupation permits you to use. Maybe you are wrestling with some personal dilemma that has you bewildered.

Whatever has driven you to the current moment – a moment when you have paused to examine the ideas contained in this book – it would appear that you are in search of *answers*. You are one of those fortunate human beings who is ready for some change, and *that* is what this book is all about: transforming the individual human life from where and what it is into where and what you desire it to *be*.

How The Process Of Change Begins

Change comes from one of two sources. First, we may be driven to change out of *desperation*. Sometimes our circumstances can become so out-of-control that we almost abandon our search for answers because our lives seem to be filled only with irresolvable *questions*. But it is this overwhelming sense of desperation that finally *drives* us to look for the solutions. Desperation is the final and inevitable result of months or years of accumulated neglect that brings us to that point in time where we find ourselves driven by urgent necessity to find immediate answers to life's accumulated challenges.

The second source that drives us to make changes in our lives is *inspiration*. Hopefully, that is where you find yourself right now – about to become sufficiently inspired to make major and dramatic changes in your life as a result of the message I am about to share with you.

Inspiration can come to us at any time and from many sources. A song can inspire us, a book can inspire us, as can an effective and moving speech. The story of someone who has succeeded in spite of difficulty can stir our emotions. Inspiration, from whatever the source, arouses feelings within us that rekindle hope, ambition and determination. It is a momentary whisper of encouragement and reassurance that causes us to become aware of our potential. We sense a spark of desire, and our minds flash from one possibility to another, each thought laden with the promise of future success and happiness. In this fleeting moment when inspiration stirs our soul we are either driven into action or we do nothing – being content to enjoy the warm feeling that is within us until, at last, the warmth moves on, taking with it the promise and the possibilities.

Wherever life finds you at the moment, whether responding to desperation or seeking inspiration, I appeal to you for your undivided attention and a promise to complete this book, not just start it. In the end, our lives will be judged not by the things that we began, but by the things that our effort and resolve brought to a successful *conclusion*.

I have used the utmost care to assemble some insights and ideas that are truly life-changing. The inspiration that I trust you will receive from this book has the capacity to alter *any* human circumstance. But in order for these ideas to work their inevitable magic in your life, you must take time in the weeks ahead to seriously contemplate the direction of your life, and to ponder the message and carefully apply the principles in the pages that follow.

Let me begin by sharing with you a few important and preliminary insights that can start you on your journey toward success and happiness.

The Key To Success And Happiness

There are always just a few important principles that account for most of the progress we make in our lives. It is these "basics" that have the greatest effect on our health, our happiness and our bank accounts. This is not to suggest that there are *only* a few life-changing ideas that will affect us, for surely there are many. What I *am* suggesting, however, is that you begin your search by focusing on the five fundamentals we will examine in this book. It is these few among the many that will account for the biggest share of the results you will achieve.

You will never be able to master *every* aspect of life. To try to become the master over every detail of your life will only lead to frustration. Instead, why not go after the few among the many; the few that will make the *most* difference; the fundamental subjects that will have the greatest impact in determining the quality of your existence?

As you look around your world for answers to the good

life, always be in search of those *few* things that make the *most* difference. If you master these basics, I can promise that you will not be disappointed with the results.

It is the basics – the fundamentals in life – that we all need to master. These are the same keys for success and happiness that have existed for the last six thousand years of recorded history. There are no *new* fundamentals for human achievement. Basics are basics, and anything else is merely an activity designed to refine or expand upon those same principles.

In any attempt to improve your current circumstances, never allow yourself to drift from those time-proven principles that have flowed from generation to generation in a steady stream to serve as the fundamentals for finding, developing and living the good life.

The Five Pieces To The Life Puzzle

If everyone reading this book were to sit down and develop their own list of the five major principles that make the most difference, we would probably have a hundred different answers to share with one another. And to some extent, all of the answers would be correct, since each of us holds certain principles in a higher light than others.

It is important to understand that the list I will be sharing with you in this book does not mean that *my* five are the *only* five to the exclusion of all others. I am neither so wise nor so presumptuous as to suggest that I have all of the answers and that my answers are the *only* answers. The principles we will cover in this book are five important concepts that are as fundamental to your success now as they were for preceeding generations. Through all my years of study and experience, through all my encounters with both success and failure, through all the conversations and associations I have had the privilege to share, it is these five principles that have remained unchallenged in their capacity to produce life-changing results.

Endurance is often the best indicator of validity and value. That is why I have invited you to take a closer look at these five enduring principles – the "basics" that seem to always be there, guiding the lives of those who have done well with life's challenges and opportunities.

I do not have the final and unchallenged answers for finding the good life. I know that there are a lot of people who claim to know *the truth*, and who suggest that they have discovered the ultimate answer to life's puzzle. But there can never be a single, ultimate answer simply because there will never be a single, ultimate question. That is why my best advice has always been to stick to the basics. And if you will give each of the basics we are about to share both time and careful attention, you are certain to be happy with the results, for they are – The Five Major Pieces To The Life Puzzle.

CHAPTER ONE

PHILOSOPHY

Philosophy is the chief cornerstone in the foundation of The Five Major Pieces To The Life Puzzle. A major factor in determining how our lives turn out is the way we choose to *think*. Everything that goes on inside the human mind in the form of thoughts, ideas and information forms our personal *philosophy*. Our philosophy then influences our habits and behavior, and this is really where it all begins.

How Our Personal Philosophy Is Formed

Our personal philosophy comes from what we *know* and from the process of how we *came* to know all that we currently know. Throughout our lives we receive input from a multitude of sources. What we know comes from school, friends, associates, media influences, home, the streets; it comes from books and the process of reading; and it comes from listening and observing. The sources of knowledge and information that have contributed to the formation of our current philosophy are virtually unlimited.

As adults all of the new information that comes our way is examined through the filter of our personal philosophy. Those concepts that seem to agree with the conclusions we have already reached are added to our storehouse of knowledge and serve to reinforce our current thinking. Those ideas that seem to contradict our beliefs are usually quickly rejected.

We are constantly in the process of checking our pre-existing beliefs for accuracy or confirmation in the light of new information. As we blend the new with the old, the result is either the strengthening of our past beliefs or the broadening of our current philosophy in light of new and valuable information about life and people.

The same beliefs that form our personal philosophy also determine our value systems. Our beliefs led us to make certain decisions about what is valuable to us as human beings. As the day goes by, we choose to *do* whatever we think is *valuable*. If someone decides to start his day at five o'clock each morning in order to take advantage of opportunities that will enable him to provide his family with more of the good things in life, then what is that person *really* doing? He is doing what his philosophy has taught him is *valuable*. Conversely, someone who chooses to sleep until noon is *also* doing what he considers to be valuable. But the *result* from the two different philosophies – from the judgements people make about what is valuable – will be drastically different.

We all have our own ideas about the things that affect our lives based on the information we have gathered over the years. Each of us has a personal view about government, education, the economy, our employer and a host of other issues. What we *think* about these issues adds to our emerging philosophy and causes us to reach certain conclusions about life and how it operates. These conclusions then lead us to make specific value judgements which determine how we will act on any given day and in any given circumstance. We have all made and will continue to make decisions based upon what we think is valuable. Whether the decisions we are making will lead us toward inevitable success or unavoidable failure depends on the information we have gathered over the years to form our personal philosophy.

Personal Philosophy Is Like The Set Of The Sail

In the process of living, the winds of circumstance blow on us all in an unending flow that touches each of our lives.

We have all experienced the blowing winds of disappointment, despair and heartbreak. Why, then, would each of us, in our own individual ship of life, all beginning at the same point, with the same intended destination in mind, arrive at such different places at the end of the journey? Have we not all sailed upon the same sea? Have we not all been blown by the same winds of circumstance and buffeted by the same turbulent storms of discontent?

What guides us to different destinations in life is determined by the way we have chosen to set our sail. The way that each of us *thinks* makes the major difference in where each of us *arrives*. The major difference is not circumstance, the *major* difference is the *set of the sail*.

The same circumstances happen to us all. We all have disappointments and challenges. We all have reversals and those moments when, in spite of our best plans and efforts, things just seem to fall apart. Challenging circumstances are not events reserved for the poor, the uneducated or the destitute. The rich *and* the poor have children who get into trouble. The rich *and* the poor have marital problems. The rich *and* the poor have the same challenges that can lead to financial ruin and personal despair. In the final analysis, it is not *what happens* that determines the quality

19

of our lives, it is what we choose to *do* when we have struggled to set the sail and then discover, after all of our efforts, that the wind has changed direction.

When the winds change, *we* must change. We must struggle to our feet once more and reset the sail in the manner that will steer us toward the destination of our own deliberate choosing. The set of the sail, how we *think* and how we *respond*, has a far greater capacity to destroy our lives than any challenges we face. How quickly and responsibly we react to adversity is far more important than the adversity itself. Once we discipline ourselves to understand this, we will finally and willingly conclude that the great challenge of life is to control the process of our own thinking.

Learning to reset the sail with the changing winds rather than permitting ourselves to be blown in a direction we did not purposely choose requires the development of a whole new discipline. It involves going to work on establishing a powerful, personal philosophy that will help to influence in a positive way all that we do and all that we think and decide. If we can succeed in this worthy endeavor, the result will be a change in the course of our income, bank account, lifestyle and relationships, and in how we feel about the things of value as well as the times of challenge. If we can alter the way we perceive, judge and decide upon the main issues of life, then we can dramatically change our lives.

How To Develop A Powerful Personal Philosophy

The greatest influence on what we decide to do with tomorrow's opportunity is not going to be circumstance, but rather what and how we *think*. What we think, and the conclusions we reach regarding life's challenges, is going to be the sum total of what we have learned until now.

The learning process plays a major role in determining our personal philosophy. Over the years we have all managed to gather up considerable knowledge. We cannot live without the information that surrounds us making an impact on how we think. The human mind is continually taking pictures and recording the sights and sounds around us. Every experience is etched into the neurons of the brain. Every word, every song, every television program, every conversation, and every book has made an electrical or chemical imprint on our mental computers. Each emotion, each thought, each activity in which we have been engaged has created a new circuit in the brain, which is linked to all of the others circuits that already existed. All that has touched our lives has been indelibly recorded, and all that we now are is the result of an accumulation of input which is intricately connected by a delicate combination of chemical and electrical impulses stored in the three-pound brain. All that has ever happened in and around us is now this uniqueness we call *self* – the individual human being.

How we use all of this information and the way in which we assemble the knowledge we have gathered forms our personal philosophy. The problem is that much of the information we have gathered has resulted in erroneous conclusions about life that can actually block the achievement of our goals. The only way to eliminate these mental barriers is to review, refine and revise our personal philosophy.

The best way to establish a new and powerful personal philosophy is to begin with an objective review of the conclusions we have drawn about life. Any conclusion that is not working *for* us may actually be working *against* us. Suppose, for example, a man has decided that his current employer is not paying him enough. His value system – based on years of accumulated information and experiences – then says, "That's not fair!" This value judgement causes him to take specific steps in retaliation. As a result, he reduces his efforts and does only those things he feels his current paycheck justifies. There is nothing wrong with this decision...provided his goal is to remain where he is, doing what he is currently doing, and getting paid what he is currently getting paid for the rest of his life.

All of our counter-productive beliefs and choices are the result of years of accumulating misinformation. We have simply been around the wrong sources and gathered up the wrong data. The decisions we are making are not wrong based on the information we have; it is the information we have that is causing us to make wrong decisions. Unfortunately, these wrong decisions are leading us further away from rather than closer toward the achievement of our goals.

The Importance Of New Information

Since it is virtually impossible to identify and erase all of the misleading information in our mental computers, the only way to change our thinking habits is to input new information. Unless we change what we know, we will continue to believe, decide and act in a manner that is contrary to our best interests.

Getting the information that success and happiness require – and getting it *accurately* – is essential. Otherwise, we will inevitably drift into ignorance, becoming deluded by our power, our prestige and our possessions.

The question is, where can we get new, accurate, and better ideas and information that will enable us to become more than we are? Fortunately, there is a wealth of positive information all around us, just waiting to be used.

Learn From Personal Experiences

One of the best ways to expand the dimensions of our knowledge is by conducting a serious review of our own past experiences. We all have a university of experience within us. The books lining the shelves of our minds were written and placed there by all that we have experienced since birth. These experiences have suggested to us that there is a right way and a wrong way to everything we do, and to every decision that *confronts* us, as well as to every obstacle that *challenges* us.

One way to learn to do something *right* is to do something *wrong*. We learn from failure as well as success. Failure must teach us, or surely success will not reward us. Past failures and errors must prompt us to amend current conduct, or the present and the future will be little more than a duplicate of the past.

We all have recorded memories of past deeds and of the subsequent rewards or consequences of those deeds. The key is to make the memories of past events our servants, lest the repetition of those events makes us their slave.

We must labor to make certain that our memories of past experiences, whether good or bad, are accurate if they are to serve us and to make the future better than our past. We must reflect on our past, reliving the moments, pondering the lessons, and refining our current conduct based on the lessons of our personal history. If we have manipulated the truth of the past, if we have tended to blame others rather than ourselves, then we are seeking an escape from reality, and we will be destined to repeat past errors and relive present difficulties.

Learn From An Outside Voice

We could all use a little coaching. In a sense, that is the purpose of this book. It brings to those in search of insights and ideas a new and objective voice. We are all capable of correcting our own errors but there is often great value in an *outside* voice – someone who can provide an objective appraisal of how we are and what we are doing, and the potential impact of our thoughts and actions on our better future.

An objective appraisal from someone whose opinion we respect (someone other than ourselves) will enable us to see things that we do not see. In our personal world we tend to see only the trees, while the objective and capable friend will more likely see the forest. Objectivity, brought to us in the form of wise counsel from one we trust and respect, can lead us to early and accurate information about ourselves and our decision-making process. It can prevent us from reaching faulty conclusions based on familiarity with our environment.

We are wise, indeed, if we discipline ourselves to take counsel and suggestion from someone who *cares*, lest life and circumstances force us to take it from one who does *not* care.

In the world of business, successful executives often turn to consultants who bring the freshness of the outside voice. Company employees can become so familiar with the problem at hand that they have lost their ability to see the solution that sits on their shoulders.

We must all make certain that we have access to our own select person or group of associates to whom we can turn for counsel when the winds have changed so often that we are no longer certain if we are still on course. Others can help us to examine our actions objectively to ensure that we have not drifted too far away from the fundamentals – the *basics*.

Learn From Other People's Experience With Failure

Other people and their personal experiences offer untold opportunities for learning. Through the experiences of others there are two valuable sources of information available; two attitudes of mind; two categories of those

24

with similar experiences but with remarkably different results. We are exposed on a daily basis to representatives of both groups. Each group seeks its own audience, and each has an effect on those who choose to listen. But both sources are important. One serves as an example to be followed, the other as an example to be *avoided* – as a *warning* to be studied, but not emulated.

We should all be students of failure. It is part of the world experience – part of the life experience. Why do we want to study the failures? So that we can learn what *not* to do.

All experiences can serve as our teachers provided we *learn* from the information and invest its value in our own lives. There are those who teach that associations with people who have not done well with their lives and their opportunities should be avoided at all cost for fear that we will learn their poor habits, and as a consequence, repeat their unfortunate mistakes. However, as someone wisely said, "Those who do not learn from the mistakes of the past are condemned to repeat them." If we ignore the lessons of the past, from whatever the source, then we may become victims of the process of trial and error. By ignoring the lessons of history, our own trials will inevitably try us and our own errors will ultimately destroy us.

It is unfortunate, perhaps, that those who fail do not teach their experiences for all to hear. If we had more opportunity to learn from the negative experiences of others, we might well save our *own* lives from certain disaster.

Learn From Other People's Success

It is worth whatever time we must take and whatever we must invest to make a study of people who do well. Gather the ideas and the information from all of the available sources. Read the books. Attend the seminars. Spend time gathering the knowledge that success requires. Study

25

the habits, the language, the manner of dress, and the disciplines of those who have succeeded.

One of the great sources of wisdom from those who have done well can be found in the many quote books that are available in bookstores. Just by reading the words of what the greatest among us (past and present) have had to say, we can come to a better understanding of the thoughts that guided the lives of those who were great enough, persuasive enough, influential enough, and successful enough to be quoted.

Capitalize On The Power Of Positive Influence

Each of us should be in constant search of people we can admire and respect, people after whom we can pattern part of our own behavior. Much of who and what we are at this very moment is a composite of the many people who have influenced us over the years. When we were younger, our idols were often storybook characters, movie stars and famous musicians. For a while we walked, dressed and even tried to talk like our heroes. As we grew older and our own unique personalities began to develop, our emulation of others became less apparent, but the influence was there nonetheless.

Regardless of our age or circumstances, we are never beyond the reach of influence. The key is to find unique human beings whose personalities and achievements stimulate, fascinate and inspire us, and then strive to assimilate their best qualities. Great projects are always built from a pattern or blueprint. In this lifetime there is no greater project than the deliberate development of our own lives. Therefore, we each need a "blueprint" – something or someone to look at and pattern ourselves after – if we want to make change and progress.

We are all being influenced by *someone*. Since this influence will determine, to some extent, the direction of

26

our lives, it is far better to *deliberately* choose the people we will permit to influence us than to allow the power of the wrong influence to weave its effect on us without our knowledge or conscious choice.

Become A Good Observer

We must never allow a day to pass without finding the answers to a list of important questions such as: What is going on in our industry? What new challenges are currently facing our government? Our community? Our neighborhood? What are the new breakthroughs, the new opportunities, the new tools and techniques that have recently come to light? Who are the new personalities that are influencing world and local opinion?

We must become good observers and astute evaluators of all that is going on around us. All events affect us, and what affects us leaves an imprint on what we will one day be and how we will one day live.

One of the major reasons why people are not doing well is because they keep trying to get *through* the day. A more worthy challenge is to try to get *from* the day. We must become sensitive enough to observe and ponder what is happening around us. Be alert. Be awake. Let life and all of its subtle messages touch us. Often, the most extraordinary opportunities are hidden among the seemingly insignificant events of life. If we do not pay attention to these events, we can easily miss the opportunities.

Become A Good Listener

It is challenging today to be a good listener. There are so many voices that want our attention, each with its own special message and each with its own special appeal. One of the best ways to deal with this important challenge is to develop the skill of *selective listening.*

Selective listening is like tuning a radio to find the station that most appeals to us. As we turn the dial, we listen for a second or two and then either keep searching or stop dialing, depending on what we have just heard. Whenever a voice calls out for our attention, we must pause for a while to ponder the message. If the message is shallow or ignorant, we must discipline ourselves to move on. We must touch the "scan" switch, and move on to the next voice so that the ignorant and shallow message does not affect us.

Everything we hear is being recorded in our mental computers and forming a new connection in the brain. We might listen to some voices for a time out of curiosity, but if the voice is not leading toward the achievement of our goals, then we must exercise great caution in how long we listen. Only when we have found a source of valuable information should we allow the message to touch us so that it might add value to who and what we already are.

One of the greatest attributes of leadership is effective communication, and learning what to *say* comes only when we have learned how to *listen.* The art of listening is an opportunity to add to our knowledge and to increase our value. The process of *speaking,* on the other hand, is the act of putting on display all – or the little – that we have learned. We must first master the art of *listening* before our spoken words will have any great value to others.

The best way to learn what to say to our children is to listen to them. We should read the books they are reading and become familiar with the messages they are receiving from a variety of sources. Listening to the information that is reaching our children will not only increase our awareness of their decision-making process, but it will also help us to talk more effectively with our children about what is valuable.

Read All The Books

All of the books that we will ever need to make us as rich, as healthy, as happy, as powerful, as sophisticated and as successful as we want to be have already been written.

People from all walks of life, people with some of the most incredible life experiences, people that have gone from pennies to fortune and from failure to success have taken the time to write down their experiences so that we might share in their wealth of knowledge. They have offered their wisdom and experience so that we can be inspired by it and instructed by it, and so that we can amend our philosophy by it. Their contributions enable us to re-set our sail based upon *their* experiences. They have handed us the gift of their insights so that we can change our plans, if need be, in order to avoid their errors. We can rearrange our lives based on their wise advice.

All of the insights that we might ever need have already been captured by others in books. The important question is this: In the last ninety days, with this treasure of information that could change our lives, our fortunes, our relationships, our health, our children and our careers for the better, how many books have we read?

Why do we neglect to read the books that can change our lives? Why *do* we complain but remain the same? Why *do* so many of us curse the effect but nourish the cause? How *do* we explain the fact that only three percent of our entire national population possess a library card – a card that would give us access to all of the answers to success and happiness we could ever want? Those who wish for the better life cannot permit themselves to miss the books that could have a major impact on how their lives turn out. The book they *miss* will not help!

And the issue is not that books are too expensive! If a person concludes that the price of *buying* the book is too great, wait until he must pay the price for *not* buying it. Wait

29

until he receives the bill for continued and prolonged ignorance.

There is very little difference between someone who *cannot* read and someone who *will not* read. The result of either is ignorance. Those who are serious seekers of personal development must remove the self-imposed limitations they have placed on their reading skills and their reading habits. There are a multitude of classes being taught on how to be a good reader and there are thousands of books on the shelves of the public libraries just waiting to be read. Reading is essential for those who seek to rise above the ordinary. We must not permit anything to stand between us and the book that could change our lives.

A little reading each day will result in a wealth of valuable information in a very short period of time. But if we fail to set aside the time, if we fail to pick up the book, if we fail to exercise the discipline, then ignorance will quickly move in to fill the void.

Those who seek a better life must first become a better person. They must continually seek after self-mastery for the purpose of developing a balanced philosophy of life, and then *live* in accordance with the dictates of that philosophy. The habit of reading is a major stepping stone in the development of a sound philosophical foundation. It is one of the *fundamentals* required for the attainment of success and happiness.

Keep A Personal Journal

In our continuing search for knowledge and understanding, there is another major discipline that will help us to capture the information around us so that our future will be better than the past: keeping a personal journal.

A journal is a gathering place for all of our observations and discoveries about life. It is our own handwritten transcript, narrated in our own words, which captures the experiences, ideas, desires and conclusions about the people and events that have touched our lives.

A journal provides us with two remarkable benefits. First, it allows us to capture all aspects of the present moment for future review. The events that take place in our lives – experiences that we live and learn from – should not just "happen;" they should be captured so that their lessons can be invested in the future. The past, when properly documented, is one of the best guides for making good decisions today that will lead to a better tomorrow.

While it is true that every event is recorded in the brain, we cannot always access the specifics surrounding those events at will. Often, the details can become blurred or distorted over time. We may remember the outcome but we may have forgotten the exact sequence of events or the decisions that were made. Without accurate information to enhance our recall of the past, we run the risk of repeating many of the same errors over and over again.

Without a journal those special moments – those milestones of emotion and experience – will be blown by the winds of our own forgetfulness into a deep corner of the mind where their value will become lost forever. The emotion of that special moment, unless captured in a journal, will soon fade. We may recall the event but we will have lost the emotion.

The second benefit of keeping a journal is that the very act of *writing* about our lives helps us to think more objectively about our actions. Writing tends to slow down the flow of information. As we pause to gather our thoughts about an event we are trying to capture on paper, we have time to ponder and to analyze the experience. We begin to see more clearly the source of our information, the facts on which we based our decisions, and the action we are taking in response to our beliefs. In other words, it is not just the event but also our personal philosophy that comes under intense scrutiny in the process of capturing our lives on paper. And it is this intense scrutiny that enables us to make refinements to our philosophy that are truly life-changing.

The discipline of keeping a journal also develops our ability to communicate more effectively. The more we practice capturing events and emotions with words, the more clearly we are able to communicate not only our ideas, but also the inherent value that exists within us.

It is an interesting fact that when President Kennedy was assassinated the personal journals of some of the country's most influential leaders captured the events of that sad day. As Air Force One cut through the sky from Dallas to Washington bearing the body of the slain president, many sat in silence recording in their journals their vivid recall of the tragedy. It was one of those rare events when history was *recorded* as it happened, not merely speculated on by historians in a distant era. That combination of written accounts later served as the basis for William Manchester's *The Death Of A President*, one of the greatest historical documents ever written.

Most men and women of accomplishment maintain and frequently review their personal journals. It is second nature to them. They seem to possess an inherent instinct that tells them that a life worth living is a life worth documenting. In fact, the process of making a deliberate and consistent habit of writing in journals may well be a major reason for their rise to above-average levels of achievement.

It is the small disciplines that lead to great accomplishments. When average people give care and attention to important matters, their own growth into greatness merely awaits the passage of time. Both small *disciplines* and minor *mistakes in judgement* tend to *accumulate*, the former to our benefit and the latter to our detriment.

Neither success nor failure occurs in a single cataclysmic event. Both are the result of the accumulation of seemingly small and insignificant decisions whose collective weight over the period of a lifetime presents the individual with his or her proportionate reward. The use or the neglect of journals is not indispensible to the achievement of success, but the use of a journal is an important piece of the life puzzle called philosophy. By neglecting the journal, the puzzle can never be truly complete.

Surely our lives are worth more than a birth certificate, a gravestone and a half-million dollars in consumed goods and services compressed between those major milestones in our lives. Journals are the tools that enable us to document the details of the failure as well as the progress of our existence, and in the process, allows us to become more than we otherwise might have been.

We are rapidly becoming a nation of passive intellects. The continued neglect of our reading and our writing skills is leading to increasingly undisciplined thinking habits. If we doubt this, we need only to look at how many of our loved ones are turning to drugs, how many of our citizens are involved in violent or white-collar crimes, and how many of our children are dropping out of school. Poor thinking habits. Poor values. Poor decisions. And if this trend remains unchecked, we could soon decline to the level of a third-rate power.

We cannot become a stronger nation until our attention to the *essentials* of life begins to change. The ability to establish more competent leadership in our government, our schools, our churches, our businesses and our communities lies in the emerging value of the individual. That is why each of us must make a commitment to develop our full human potential, one discipline at a time, one book at a time, and one small entry in our journal at a time. Only by actively pursuing new knowledge can we sufficiently refine our personal philosophy and change not only our own lives, but also the lives of those around us.

33

The Decision-Making Process

Whenever a new idea comes our way we subsconsciously place this idea on our mental scales and weigh it to determine what level of action we need to take on the idea. Those ideas that measure high on our scale receive immediate attention; those that measure low on our scale receive only minimal or infrequent notice.

Whatever level of action we determine to be correct will ultimately be decided by our *philosophy*. If we have failed to gather adequate knowledge, or if we have failed to refine or add to the knowledge we possess, then a significant number of our decisions may move us away from success rather than toward it. If we are inclined to spend major time on minor things, or even major *money* on minor things, then it is essential for us to take a closer look at our decision-making process.

The world is filled with those whose decisions are destined to destroy their chances for success. Those who do not operate from a sound philosophy often do that which they should have left undone and leave undone that which they should have *done*. They fail to set goals and establish priorities. They vacillate between one decision and another. They sense that they should be doing *something*, but lack the discipline to convert this awareness into action.

Every day is filled with dozens of personal crossroads - moments when we are called upon to make a decision regarding minor as well as major questions. It is important to remember that each and every one of the choices we make during these moments of decision charts a path leading to some future destination. Just as the sum total of our past decisions has led us to our current circumstances, the decisions we make today will lead us to the rewards or the regrets of the future.

Choices. Decisions. Selections. Each provides us with

an opportunity to determine the quality of our future. And each demands that we prepare in advance for the decision that is to be made. In those moments of choice, it is the knowledge we have acquired and the philosophy we have developed from this knowledge that will either serve us or destroy us.

That is why we must be found constantly preparing for the unanticipated confrontation with important choices. Only through careful mental preparation can we consistently make wise choices. What we *think* determines what we believe; what we *believe* influences what we *choose*; what we choose defines what we *are*; and what we are attracts what we *have*. If we are not happy with where our past decisions have led us, then the place to start is with our current thinking process. As we add new knowledge, we will begin to refine our philosophy. As our beliefs change, so too will our choices. And from better choices come better results.

The development of a sound philosophy prepares us for making sound decisions. Like the architect, we must learn to see in our minds the result we wish to achieve, and then go to work on building a solid foundation to support this vision. Once the vision is clearly defined and the foundation has been firmly established, then the choices required to complete the structure are easily and wisely made.

The Formula For Failure

Failure is not a single, cataclysmic event. We do not fail overnight. Failure is the inevitable result of an *accumulation* of poor thinking and poor choices. To put it more simply, *failure is nothing more than a few errors in judgement repeated every day.*

Now why would someone make an error in judgement and then be so foolish as to *repeat* it every day?

The answer is *because he or she does not think that it matters.*

35

On their own, our daily acts do not seem that important. A minor oversight, a poor decision, or a wasted hour generally don't result in an instant and measurable impact. More often than not, we escape from any immediate consequences of our deeds.

If we have not bothered to read a single book in the past ninety days, this lack of discipline does not seem to have any immediate impact on our lives. And since nothing drastic happened to us after the first ninety days, we repeat this error in judgement for another ninety days, and on and on it goes. Why? Because it *doesn't seem to matter*. And herein lies the great danger. Far worse than not reading the books is not even realizing that it matters!

Those who eat too many of the wrong foods are contributing to a future health problem, but the joy of the moment overshadows the consequence of the future. It does not *seem* to matter. Those who smoke too much or drink too much go on making these poor choices year after year after year...because it doesn't *seem* to matter. But the pain and regret of these errors in judgement have only been delayed for a future time. Consequences are seldom instant; instead, they accumulate until the inevitable day of reckoning finally arrives and the price must be paid for our poor choices— choices that didn't *seem* to matter.

Failure's most dangerous attribute is its subtlety. In the short term those little errors don't *seem* to make any difference. We do not *seem* to be failing. In fact, sometimes these accumulated errors in judgement occur throughout a period of great joy and prosperity in our lives. Since nothing terrible happens to us, since there are no instant consequences to capture our attention, we simply drift from one day to the next, repeating the errors, thinking the wrong thoughts, listening to the wrong voices and making the wrong choices. The sky did not fall in on us yesterday, therefore the act was probably harmless. Since it seemed to have no measurable consequence, it is probably safe to repeat.

But we must become better educated than that!

If at the end of the day when we made our first error in judgement the sky *had* fallen in on us, we undoubtedly would have taken immediate steps to ensure that the act would never be repeated again. Like the child who places his hand on a hot burner despite his parents' warnings, we would have had an instantaneous experience accompanying our error in judgement.

Unfortunately, failure does not shout out its warnings as our parents once did. This is why it is imperative to refine our philosophy in order to be able to make better choices. With a powerful, personal philosophy guiding our every step, we become more aware of our errors in judgement and more aware that each error really *does* matter.

The Formula For Success

Like the formula for failure, the formula for success is easy to follow:

A few simple disciplines practiced every day.

Now here is an interesting question worth pondering: How can we change the *errors* in the formula for failure into the *disciplines* required in the formula for success? The answer is by making the future an important part of our current philosophy.

Both success and failure involve future consequences, namely the inevitable rewards or unavoidable regrets resulting from past activities. If this is true, why don't more people take time to ponder the future? The answer is simple: They are so caught up in the current moment that *it doesn't seem to matter.* The problems and the rewards of today are so absorbing to some human beings that they never pause long enough to think about tomorrow.

37

But what if we did develop a new discipline to take just a few minutes every day to look a little further down the road? We would then be able to foresee the impending consequences of our current conduct. Armed with that valuable information, we would be able to take the necessary action to change our errors into new success-oriented disciplines. In other words, by disciplining ourselves to see the future in advance, we would be able to change our thinking, amend our errors and develop new habits to replace the old.

A Few Simple Disciplines Practiced Every Day

One of the exciting things about the formula for success is that the results are almost immediate. As we voluntarily change daily errors into daily *disciplines*, we experience positive results in a very short period of time. When we change our diet, our health improves noticeably in just a few weeks. When we start exercising, we feel a new vitality almost immediately. When we begin reading, we experience a growing awareness and a new level of self-confidence. Whatever new discipline we begin to practice daily will produce exciting results that will drive us to become even better at developing new disciplines.

The real magic of new disciplines is that they will cause us to amend our *thinking*. If we were to start today to read the books, keep a journal, attend the classes, listen more and observe more, then today would be the first day of a new life leading to a better future. If we were to start today to try harder, and in every way make a conscious and consistent effort to change subtle and deadly errors into constructive and rewarding disciplines, we would never again settle for a life of existence – not once we have tasted the fruits of a life of substance!

There are those who would lead us to believe that we do not need the disciplines in order to change our lives – that all a person needs is a little motivation. But "motivation" is not how people change their lives. To change a *life* we must first change our thinking habits. If a person is a fool and becomes motivated, he merely becomes a motivated fool.

To change ourselves from how we are to how we want to be, we must begin with those few basics that affect the way we *think*. We can greatly change the course of our lives by spending more time and making a greater conscious effort to refine our personal philosophy.

The exciting thing is that we will not have to change all that much for the results to very quickly change for us.

Disciplines Tend To Multiply

All disciplines affect each other. Every new discipline affects not only the discipline that we have already begun to practice, but also the disciplines we will soon adopt.

Everything affects everything else. Some things affect us more than others, but everything we do has an effect on everything *else* we do. Not to think so is naive. This is where those little subtle *errors* can come from – from not knowing the effect that our errors are having on our lives over an extended period of time.

There is a tendency for each of us to give ourselves license to continue an undisciplined act. We tell ourselves "This is the only area in which I allow myself to be weak." But this type of thinking is the beginning of delusion, for each undisciplined act tends to open the floodgates leading to other breakdowns in the chain of self-discipline. The license we give to ourselves to wander even momentarily outside the boundaries of self-control establishes a *subtle tendency*, and the passing of time will eventually cause other self-imposed disciplines to erode.

Since every discipline affects every *other* discipline, we must be careful with all of them. We cannot allow ourselves the luxury of indulging *any* error day in and day out.

39

Remember, every liberty we give ourselves to continue with an error has an effect on all of our other good habits, which in time has an effect on our future *performance*.

But here is the positive side. Every *new* discipline affects all of our *other* disciplines. Every new discipline that we impose on ourselves will affect the rest of our personal performance in a positive way.

The key is to keep looking for every small discipline we can find that will cause us to refine our thinking, amend our errors and improve our results. We must continue looking for even the most insignificant of those errors in judgement that could be converted into a new discipline. Once the discipline cycle is started, our errors will begin to feel the effect, leaving tangible rewards in their wake as they make a hasty retreat.

Success And Happiness Are Easy To Achieve

Taken one step at a time, all of the things that success and happiness require are actually quite *easy* to do. Changing from errors to disciplines is easy, as is going from failure to success. The reason why it is so easy is because we can do it, and anything we have the ability to do is always easy. Now, we may have to work hard at the daily discipline part of the equation, but reaching out with our talents to embrace success and its rewards is very easy to do.

But if it is so easy, why don't more of us do it?

Because while it is easy to do the things that success and happiness require, it is *also* easy *not* to do them.

The Danger Of Neglect

The things that are easy to do are also easy *not* to do. The primary reason most people are not doing as well as they could and should can be summed up in a single word: neglect.

40

It is not the lack of money – banks are full of money. It is not the lack of opportunity – America continues to offer the most unprecedented and abundant opportunities of any nation in the last six thousand years of recorded history. It is not the lack of books – libraries are full of books...and they are free! It is not the schools – the classrooms are full of good teachers. We have plenty of ministers, leaders, counselors and advisors.

Everything we would ever need to become rich and powerful and sophisticated is within our reach. The major reason that so few take advantage of all that we have is, simply, *neglect*.

Many of us have heard the expression "An apple a day keeps the doctor away." We may debate the validity of this familiar quotation, but what if it were true? If by performing that one simple act – that one simple discipline – we could be more healthy and alert and active throughout our lives, then would it not make sense and would it not be easy to eat that apple every day?

Assuming the quotation is true, why don't more of us eat an apple a day – every day – to maintain our health? If it is that easy, and there is such a tremendous reward attached to this discipline, why do we *not* do it? Because the things that are easy to *do* are also easy *not* to do. That is how subtle failure is. Failure is largely a function of neglect. We fail to do the small things that we should do, and this seemingly insignificant license carries over to those things that *are* important to do. Small neglects have a way of becoming major oversights with the passage of enough time.

Neglect is like an infection. Left unchecked it will spread throughout our entire system of disciplines and eventually lead to a complete breakdown of a potentially joy-filled and prosperous human life.

Not doing the things we know we *should* do causes us to feel guilty and guilt leads to an erosion of self-confidence. As our self-confidence diminishes, so does the level of our activity. And as our activity diminishes, our results inevitably decline. And as our results suffer, our attitude beings to weaken. And as our attitude begins the slow shift from positive to negative, our self-confidence diminishes even more...and on and on it goes. Failure to do the things that we could and should do results in the creation of a negative spiral, which once started, is difficult to stop.

Learn To Listen To The Right Voice

Why are we so frequently inclined to do the things that are least important but so reluctant to do the essential things that success and happiness demand? What *is* that voice that whispers to us, "Just let it all slide. Why worry about all that discipline nonsense?" It is the voice of *negativity*, a voice that has grown increasingly stronger over the years as a result of being around the wrong influences, thinking the wrong thoughts, developing the wrong philosophy and making the wrong decisions.

Part of the solution to quieting the voice of negativity is learning to listen to the still, small voice of success which resides inside each of us. The voice of success is constantly struggling to be heard above the loud promptings of the voice of failure. Our own free agency allows us to follow whichever voice we choose. Everytime we allow ourselves to succumb to the voice of the dark side of life, and are persuaded to repeat errors instead of mastering new disciplines, the voice of negativity grows stronger. Conversely, each time we listen to the urgings of the voice of success, and are persuaded to turn off the television and pick up a book, to open our journals and record our thoughts, or to spend a quiet moment pondering where our current actions may be leading us, the voice of success responds to these new disciplines and grows in strength and volume as each day passes. For each new discipline, another step forward.

We can never *totally* eradicate the voice of failure from

within us. It will always be there, urging us to think and feel and act in a way that is contrary to our own best interests. But we can effectively silence this destructive influence by developing a sound philosophy and a positive attitude about life and our future.

Creating a new philosophy is easy to do. Making new and better decisions is easy to do. Developing a new attitude is easy to do. All of the worthwhile and rewarding things we have covered in this chapter are easy to do, but the major challenge – the one that could leave us with pennies instead of fortune and trinkets instead of treasures – is that it is also easy *not* to do.

We must keep a watchful eye on the subtle differences between success and failure, and be ever mindful of the inner urgings that would have us repeating costly errors rather than developing new disciplines.

We must each make our own conscious decision to reach out for the good life through the refinement of our thoughts and the careful examination of the potential consequences of our accumulated errors. We must not allow ourselves to think that the errors do not matter. *They do.* We must not allow ourselves to assume that a lack of discipline in one small area of our lives will not make a difference. *It will.* And we must not allow ourselves to believe that we can have all that we want to have and become all that we wish to be without making any changes in the way we think about life. *We must.*

The journey toward the good life begins with a serious commitment to changing any aspect of our current philosophy that has the capacity to come between us and our dreams. The remaining pieces of the puzzle of life can be of little value if we have not first made the firm resolve to do something with *this* piece of the puzzle.

Everything is within our reach if we will read the books, use the journals, practice the disciplines, and wage a new and vigorous battle against neglect. These are some of the fundamental activities that lead not only to the development of a new philosophy, but to a new life filled with joy and accomplishment. Each new and positive activity weakens the grip of failure and steers us ever closer to the destination of our choice. Each new, disciplined step taken toward success strengthens our philosophical posture and increases our chances of achieving a well-balanced life. But the first step in realizing this worthy achievement lies in becoming the master of our ship and the captain of our soul by developing a sound personal *philosophy*.

CHAPTER TWO

ATTITUDE

Our lives are greatly affected by what we *know* since what we *know* determines the *decisions* we will make.

Just as we are affected by what we know, we are also affected by how we *feel*.

While philosophy deals essentially with the *logical* side of life – information and thinking habits – attitude focuses primarily on the *emotional* issues that affect our existence. What we *know* determines our philosophy. How we *feel* about what we know determines our attitude.

It is our emotional nature that governs most of our daily conduct in our personal and business worlds. It is the emotional aspect of our experiences that determines our behavior. How we each *feel* about life's events is a powerful force that can either freeze us in our tracks or inspire us to take immediate action on any given day.

Like thoughts, emotions have the capacity to propel us toward future fortune or future disaster. The feelings that we carry within us about people, our work, our homes, our finances, and about the world around us collectively form our *attitude*. With the right attitude human beings can move mountains. With the wrong attitude they can be crushed by the smallest grain of sand.

Having the right attitude is an essential prerequisite for success and happiness. The right attitude is one of the fundamentals of the good life. That is why we must constantly examine our feelings about our role in the world and about our possibilities for achieving our dreams. The feelings that we have affect our prevailing attitude, and it is our prevailing attitude that ultimately determines the quality of our lives.

Attitude is a major determining factor in how our lives turn out. Since everything in life affects everything else, we must make a careful study of everything and everyone that might be having the wrong affect on our current attitude.

The Past

Having a healthy and mature attitude about the past can make a major difference in anyone's life. One of the best ways to approach the past is to use it as a *school*, not as a *weapon*. We must not beat ourselves to death with past mistakes, faults, failures and losses. The events of the past, both good and bad, are all part of the life experience. For some, the past may have been a harsh teacher. But we must remember to let the past educate us and bring the *value* of its experience into our lives. It is *easy* to allow the past to overwhelm us. But the good news is that it is also *easy* to allow the past to *instruct* us and to increase our value.

Part of the miracle of our future lies in the past. Past lessons. Past errors. Past successes. The collective experiences of all that has happened to us can either be our master or our servant. That is why it is so important to gather up the lessons of the past and invest them in the future. If we can establish that kind of intelligent approach to the past, we can dramatically change the course of the next twelve months. Each of us will be *somewhere* in the next twelve months; the question we must ask ourselves is *where*?

Developing a new philosophy about the past is the key to changing our current attitude. Until we have finally accepted the fact that there is nothing we can do to change the past, our feelings of regret and remorse and bitterness will prevent us from designing a better future with the opportunity that is before us *today*.

How effectively we use the present is largely determined by our attitude about the past. Until we amend our philosophy, we cannot repair our attitude. And if we cannot repair our attitude, our future is going to be filled with the same sense of regret and remorse and bitterness that currently has us by the throat. We cannot move forward into a brighter future until we have closed the door on the darkness of the past.

The Present

The current moment is where our better future begins. The past gave us a wealth of memories and experiences, and the present gives us a chance to use them wisely.

The present brings us an opportunity to create an exciting future. But the promise of the future demands that we pay a price in the present. The opportunity of the current moment must be embraced or the rewards of the future will be withheld.

Our goals and ambitions of the past are bringing to us *present* rewards. If our current rewards are small, then our past efforts were small. And if today's effort is small, the *future* reward will be small as well.

Today brings to each of us 1,440 minutes; 86,400 ticks of the clock. Both the poor and the wealthy have the same 24 hours of opportunity. Time favors no one. Today merely says, "Here I am. What are you going to do with me?"

How well we use each day is largely a function of attitude. With the right attitude we can seize *this* day and make it a point of new beginning. Today does not care about yesterday's failures or tomorrow's regrets. It merely offers the same precious gift – another 24 hours – and hopes that we will use it wisely.

The greatest opportunity today brings with it is the opportunity to begin the process of *change*. Today – the *present* – is the moment when we can inaugurate our new life. It can be a new administration coming into office, a new voice coming into power. It can be a new "change of mind" – a new *attitude* adopted about who we are, what we are, what we want and what we are going to do. Today can also be exactly like yesterday, and the day before, and the day before... It is all a question of *attitude*.

The Future

Our attitude about the *future* is also of great importance. In their classic, *Lessons of History*, Will and Ariel Durant wrote:

> "To endure what *is*, we must remember what *was*,
> and dream of things as they will one day *be*."

Our attitude *about* the future depends on our ability to *see* the future. Each of us has the inherent ability to dream, design and experience the future through the power of an imaginative inner-eye. Whatever the mind has the capacity to *imagine*, it also has the ability to *create*.

Just as the body instinctively knows how to perform the miracle of *health*, the mind instinctively knows how to perform the miracle of *wealth*.

All Things Must Be Finished Before They Can Be Started

Everything in the world around us was finished in the mind of its creator before it was started. The houses we live in, the cars we drive, our clothing, our furnishings – all of these things began with an idea. Each idea was then studied, refined and perfected, either mentally or on paper, before the first nail was driven or the first piece of cloth was cut. Long before the idea was converted into a physical reality, the mind had clearly envisioned the finished product.

The human being designs his or her own future through much the same process. We begin with an idea about how the future will be. Over a period of time we refine and perfect the vision. Before long, our every thought, decision and activity are all working in harmony to bring into existence what we have mentally concluded about the future.

This is why having the right attitude about both past and present circumstances is so important. When we have a healthy attitude about the past and constructive feelings about ourselves and our present opportunities, we subconsciously guide ourselves toward the achievement of our dreams. However, when we are filled with regrets about the past and concerns about the present, then we subconsciously lead ourselves toward a future that is very much like the past we have just left behind.

The thoughts and feelings we allow ourselves to have *today* are crucial, for they are contributing to our future. What that future holds will simply be a mirror image of our current philosophy and attitude about life.

Designing A Better Future

There is a very special emotional magic that takes place when we design the future and set new goals with a

49

specific purpose in mind. As we see the future clearly in our mind's eye, we experience a level of excitement in anticipation of the day when all that we dream will become a reality. The more clearly we see the vision of the future, the more we are able to borrow from its inspiration. This borrowed inspiration finds its way into our conversations, our energy level, our relationships and our attitude. The more excited we become by our future dreams, the easier it is to develop the necessary disciplines and make the refinements to our philosophy. In other words, our dreams inspire us to think and act and feel and become exactly the kind of person we must be to realize our dreams.

If we are intelligent enough to invest our experiences of the past, and wise enough to "borrow" the excitement and inspiration of the future by clearly *seeing* that future in the "mind's eye," then past experiences and future excitement become today's servant. The finished product we foresee guides us in our present efforts, making the attainment of the better future an inevitable conclusion. We become *pulled* by the future and *guided* by the past because we have chosen to take intelligent action in the present.

The unique ability we have for investing our past experiences and borrowing inspiration from the future is an incredible force. And the good news is – anyone can do it! We all have the capacity for designing the future in *advance* so that when the new day arrives it is more than it might have been simply because we used part of our past and our future to create it.

The power of the future is an *awesome* force. What can *be* has the power to drive us to do all that we can *do*.

The Future Always Carries Its Own Price Tag

The promise of the future is not free. There is a price to be paid for any future reward. The price the future exacts from us involves discipline, labor, consistency and a burning desire to make the future better than either the past or the present. Those are the price tags of progress, but the price gets *easy* when the *promise* becomes clear. When the *end* becomes attractive, we become keenly interested in the *means*. We must see and want the promise with an insatiable desire, or the price it requires will overcome our wishes, and we will fall back to where we once were.

If we are sincere about wanting a better life, we must ask ourselves what we see in our future that is fueling our fires of confidence and excitement. How much of that future do we actually *see* and *believe*, deep within our own souls, that we will achieve? Is it clear enough in our minds and hearts to drive us out of bed each morning and keep us up late each night? Are we so locked in on the target we have selected that we can brush away any obstacle and disappointment? In our desire to change ourselves and our current circumstances are we fully prepared to go over, under, around and through whatever challenge life throws at us?

We cannot move *casually* into a better future. We cannot *casually* pursue the goal we have set for ourselves. A goal that is casually pursued is not a goal; at best it is a *wish*, and wishes are little more than self-delusion. Wishes are an anesthetic to be used by the unambitious, a narcotic that dulls their awareness of their own desperate condition.

It is possible to *plan* our future so carefully and so clearly that when the plan is complete, we can become so inspired by it, it will become our "magnificent obsession."

The challenge is to let this obsession fuel the fire that heats our talent and our skills to the boiling point so that we are propelled into a whole new future.

As we become serious about designing the future in advance, we derive an immediate emotional benefit. The future is exciting! The more clearly we see the future and the more keenly we sense its promise, the more positive our attitude becomes that we can and will achieve our dreams.

51

It is this new attitude that will provide us with renewed ambition for progress and the faith that we really *can* move mountains.

We Cannot Succeed By Ourselves

Everyone needs other people to help them in achieving their dreams. We all need each other. In the business world we need each other's market and ideas. In the personal world we need each other's inspiration and cooperation. The attitude of other people affects *each* of us and the attitude of each of us has the capacity to affect *all* of us.

The American Pledge of Allegiance, and its thirty-one words that we often repeat as an expression of our loyalty, begins with "I" and concludes with "all." That is what America is all about: you and I working together to create greatness. We are uniquely influenced and affected by *each other* in our pursuit of the American dream.

We become a powerful force when *each* of us understands how powerful *all* of us are and when *all* of us understand how valuable *each* of us is.

What can *all* of us do? The most incredible things. We can go to the moon and beyond. We can solve the mysteries of disease, diminish famine and suffering, enhance the number and quality of opportunities available for everyone, and create that which does not yet exist that will improve the conditions of all mankind. We can bring peace where there was once war, and friendship where animosity once prevailed. We can explore the heavens, examine the ocean depths, and investigate the unlimited creativity and capacity of the human mind. Nothing is beyond our reach, for nothing is beyond our imagination, and imagination is the starting point for all progress.

The contribution of *all of us* is so important to *each of us*. All of us in the company, the church, the family, the community and the classroom are intricately connected to each of us.

Our attitude about that interconnection of each of us to all of us and all of us to each of us has great influence on our future. As John Donne once wrote -

"No man is an island, entire of itself; every man is a piece of the continent, a part of the main. ...Any man's death diminishes me, because I am involved in mankind; and therefore never send to know for whom the bell tolls; it tolls for *thee*."

Appreciating Self-Worth Is The Beginning Of Progress

What would happen if we all put our minds to work and read the books, took the classes and discovered new ways to refine our philosophy? What would happen if we all developed a new attitude about the past, the present and the future? What would happen if we all changed our feelings about one another and the importance of each individual to our collective destiny? If we did all that, just imagine what an incredible effect this would have on our future!

The exciting thing is that each of us already has enough mental, spiritual, intellectual and creative power to do all that we could ever dream of doing. Everyone has it! We just need to become more aware of all that we already have and spend more time refining all that we already are, and then put it to work for us.

What stops us from recognizing our inherent gifts and talents is a poor attitude about ourselves. Why are we so quick to see the value in others and yet so reluctant to see it in ourselves? Why are we always ready to applaud someone else's accomplishment and yet so shy about recognizing our own?

53

How We Feel About Ourselves Is A Matter Of Choice

How we see ourselves is a matter of choice, not circumstances, and the major determining factor in how we feel about ourselves lies in our personal *philosophy*.

If we were to ask some people why they feel the way they do about certain issues, we would probably discover that the reason why they feel the way they do is because they really don't *know* a great deal about those issues. Lacking all of the information, they form conclusions based on the bits and pieces that have come their way. With their limited knowledge, they often make poor decisions about how things are. If they *knew* better, they would *think* better. In other words, they would reach better conclusions simply by increasing their knowledge.

And here is another part of the equation: If they *knew* better, they would *feel* better. Why would they feel better? Because they would begin to make better decisions, and from those better decisions they would start making better choices, which would produce better results.

Our attitude is shaped by decisions and choices we have made based on the knowledge we have acquired. Imagine the artist who wants to paint a masterpiece, but who has only a few colors on his palette. He may have the desire to create a masterpiece, but he lacks the variety of colors which the painting of a true masterpiece requires. This is what happens to human beings with limited knowledge. They lack the "mental colors" with which to create a complete picture.

If there is one area in the knowledge department where we cannot afford to be lacking, it is knowledge and awareness of our own uniqueness. We do not *feel* better about ourselves for the simple reason that we do not really *know* ourselves. For if we truly knew ourselves – our strengths, our abilities, our resources, our depth of feeling, our sense of humor, our unique accomplishments – we would never again doubt our ability to create a better future.

Each of us is unique. There is no one else in the world quite like us. We are the only ones who can do the special things we do. And what we do *is* special. We may not win great awards or public acclaim for our deeds, but we make the world a better place because of them. We make our families stronger, our offices more efficient and our community more prosperous because we are who we are.

Changing how we feel about ourselves begins with developing a new philosophy about the value of each human being – ourselves included! Most of us are so busy living our lives that we never pause long enough to appreciate all that we do in a given day. We have no appreciation of ourselves simply because we have no *awareness* of ourselves. Self-knowledge is a critical part of the life puzzle. As we learn more about who we are, we begin to make better choices and decisions for ourselves and about ourselves. And as we have already suggested, as our choices improve, so do our results, and as our results improve, so does our attitude.

How We Feel Is Influenced By Our Associations

The people with whom we choose to associate are a major source of what we know and how we feel.

There are three major questions which those in search of a better life must constantly ask themselves:

QUESTION #1: Who am I around?

It pays to take a survey once in a while of those people who touch our lives on a daily basis and to mentally weigh the effect these members of our *inner circle* might be having on us. What reputation do they have with those who are productive, knowledgeable and respected? What is the level of their own past accomplishments? What is the depth of their knowledge? Do they understand the value and importance of attitude, goals and personal development? How many books have they read in the past ninety days? How many classes or seminars have they attended to develop new skills or to refine their current abilities? How do they look upon the value of virtues such as commitment, persistence, fairness, patience and diligent activity? What is it about them that makes their advice, opinions and counsel valuable?

Hopefully our inner circle does not consist of people whose strongest assets are an unlimited supply of jokes and a variety of distorted opinions.

Those who can reach us and affect us on a daily basis should inspire us, not spread the seeds of doubt and dissent with their pessimism, complaining and ridicule of others. Maintaining a positive attitude in the face of life's challenges is difficult enough without *this* kind of influence in our lives.

QUESTION #2: *What effect are they having?*

That's a legitimate question. Where do *they* have *us* going? How have they got us talking? What have they got us thinking, reading and doing? What influence are they having on our ability to perform well and to grow, and to feel good about what we are doing? Most important of all – what do they have us *becoming?*

It is easy to let the wrong people slip into our lives. That is why we must take a close look at this circle of influence. We must frequently assure ourselves that the wrong voices of influence have not invaded our garden of opportunity, sowing seeds of negativity and doubt.

Delicate as this subject may be, we have all probably accumulated a few close friends whose attitudes and habits are damaging to our chances for success and happiness.

They may be nice people, with the best intentions, but if their effect is wrong, then we may have to make some difficult choices. In an effort to protect ourselves from the wrong influences, we may be forced to walk away from people we have known for many years in order to develop more positive and motivating friendships.

QUESTION #3: Is that acceptable?

Re-evaluating our associations can be a difficult issue. Progress is often painful, but so are the consequences of allowing other people to exercise undue influence upon us.

Sometimes it is helpful to remember that it is not just *our* attitude that we are attempting to protect and nurture, but the future well-being of others as well. If we are strong, we can help others to change and to improve their lives. If we are not, then the influence of certain people can make our own progress difficult, if not impossible.

In order to protect our better future we must have the courage to *disassociate* whenever necessary. That may not be an *easy* choice, but it may be a *necessary* one. All of us become careless on occasion, and the wrong people, the wrong opportunity, or the wrong thoughts can find their way into our lives. The key is to learn to recognize the effect and to take the necessary steps to minimize or eliminate the source.

Why take such drastic action? Because the negative influence is too powerful and too threatening. Never underestimate the power of influence. The reason why influence is so powerful is because it has the capacity to *change* us, and change can be difficult to reverse, particularly if it is change for the worse.

Like failure, influence is *subtle*. We would never allow someone to deliberately push us off the course we have set for ourselves. But if we are not careful, we might inadvertently permit someone to *nudge* us in the wrong direction a little each day. They may be so effective at these nudges that we don't even notice what is happening...until it is too late and the damage is done. We might even think the person who is doing the nudging is a friend.

A nudge here, a nudge there, and as time passes, we soon find ourselves looking around and saying, "What am I doing *here*? This is not where I meant to be!" We wind up spending weeks or months or even *years* merely trying to return to the course we had *thought* we were on before our nudging friend came by, subtly destroying our future with the power of undue influence.

Disassociation is not something to be treated lightly. It must be done carefully and thoughtfully. But if we are sincere about changing ourselves and designing a better future, we are obligated to distance ourselves from those who are having the wrong effect on us. The price of *not* doing it is simply too enormous.

The Value Of Limited Association

Another option for protecting our attitude is *limited association*. We cannot avoid talking to co-workers or refuse to visit with certain relatives for the rest of our lives. But we can limit the time we actually spend with these people, and in so doing, limit their ability to influence us.

There are some people with whom we can spend a few minutes, but not a few hours. There are some with whom we can spend a few hours, but not a few days. Not when the achievement of our dreams is at stake.

Excessive influence is *undue influence*. We can sometimes avoid having to end a relationship with a friend whose negative influence is affecting us by carefully limiting the amount of time we spend with that individual. But we must be very careful even with limited association. *Occasional* influences are very subtle because they can have an *accumulative* effect that is difficult to see. We must always remember that failure is the slow and imperceptible accumulation of small errors in judgement repeated on a daily basis over a prolonged period of time.

In our personal and business worlds about eighty percent of the people with whom we associate – the vast majority – will account for only about twenty percent of the results we achieve. Conversely, about *twenty* percent – the clear minority – will produce *eighty* percent of the good results. And here is a strange but valuable insight to go along with that interesting fact: It is the eighty percent group (who only produce twenty percent of the good results) that will try to capture eighty percent of our time, while the twenty percent group (who produce *eighty* percent of the good results) will receive only *twenty* percent of our time.

The challenge here should be clear. We should discipline ourselves to spend eighty percent of our time with the twenty percent who are helping us to produce *eighty* percent of the results, and *twenty* percent of our time with the eighty percent who are producing only twenty percent of the results. This is not an easy assignment. Often those in the larger group are masters at gaining access to those who are striving to do well. They have the capacity, if we are not careful, to steal away about eighty percent of our valuable time. If we allow it, they will be like the camel who pokes his nose under the tent. Left unchecked, the camel will slowly inch his way *inside* the tent and we will soon find ourselves on the *outside*.

Those who seek fortune and happiness must become aware of how the eighty percent group operates. Most are good people, but they are caught up in the search for the *how-to* of success and have not yet captured the importance of the *why-to*. They do not know that reasons come first and that answers come second. They have not yet discovered that when the human mind locks on to a personal *obsession*, it does not need a book of instructions or a training class on how to take advantage of opportunity.

In this world of opportunity mixed with challenge, there are those who want to know so that they might *see,* and there are those who think they *see* even though they do not yet *know.*

There are those in the great multitude whose attention to progress and personal development has been greatly neglected. If we were fortunate enough to have discovered gold, and sought a few close friends with whom we wished to share our discovery, some would likely disappoint us.

If we asked for their assistance and their labor in exchange for part of our fortune, some would find fault with the terms of the offer.

Some would complain about the splinters from the cheap shovels and the blisters brought about by their labors.

Some would complain about the distance between the comfort of their homes and the location of the gold mine.

Some would complain about how bad the tax bite will be after all the work is done and how unfair it all is.

Still others would complain because someone else was getting more than their fair shair.

And others still would condemn us for showing favoritism to other friends.

Personal growth is not always an easy matter, but the worst days experienced by those who give attention to the affairs of self-development are better than the best days of those who do not.

We must not delay our commitment to finding our own personal "gold mine" in life simply because of the opinions of others whom we deem to be worthy and deserving friends, but whose impact on our attitude and our self-confidence steals away too much of our spirit and dampens too much of our desire. We are obligated to limit or remove the undue influences of those who are having the wrong effect on us. Otherwise we risk losing our own vision due to the pessimism of those who do not share our desire to experience more of the good life.

The Value Of Expanded Association

Another choice we can make regarding our associations and their potential for impact on our feelings is *expanded association*. Very simply, this means finding people who have value, and arranging our lives in order to be able to spend more time with them.

Even a *small* amount of time can make a great deal of difference when it is spent with the right people – people who educate, encourage, inspire and assist us in moving in the right direction.

It is better to spend a little time with the right people than to spend a lot of time with the wrong people. By expanding our association to include more of the *right* people, and closing the doors to exclude or limit more of the *wrong* people, we expose ourselves to new and better sources of influence.

New And Better Sources Of Influence

Sources of new information and ideas that can have a dramatic impact on our attitude are within everyone's reach. The information that success requires can come from a variety of sources. The information is all around us, if we will just begin the search.

Even if we cannot get around the right people in person, we can always have access to them through their spoken words. There is a wealth of information and inspiration available to us all through audiocassette tapes. These tape programs give us new insights into goal-setting, attitude development, time management, leadership skills, financial management and a multitude of important subjects. By listening to these new voices of inspiration as we drive to and from work, we find that new seeds of progress will enter our minds causing us to think new and more constructive thoughts. The voices from the tapes will bring more good into the lives of those who listen than will the voices from the radio.

In order to be effective the tapes must be *used repeatedly*. Their messages must be listened to again and again to give these new voices time to influence us. *Repetition* is the mother of skill.

Finding new voices to inspire us is not a matter of skill or luck, it is a question of attitude. It is the *student* who must seek out the teacher, for rarely does a good idea interrupt us. Success moves toward those who *search* for progress, not toward those who need or want its rewards.

Attitude Is Everything

The process of human change begins *within* us. We all have tremendous potential. We all desire good results from our efforts. Most of us are willing to work hard and to pay the price that success and happiness demand.

Each of us has the ability to put our unique human potential into action and to acquire a desired result. But the one thing that determines the *level* of our potential, that produces the *intensity* of our activity, and that predicts the quality of the result we receive is our *attitude*.

Attitude determines how much of the future we are allowed to see. It decides the size of our dreams and influences our determination when we are faced with new challenges. No other person on earth has dominion over our attitude. People can affect our attitude by teaching us poor thinking habits or unintentionally misinforming us or providing us with negative sources of influence, but no one can control our attitude unless we voluntarily surrender that control.

No one else "makes us angry." We make *ourselves*

angry when we surrender control of our attitude. What someone else may have done is irrelevant. *We* choose, not they. They merely put our attitude to a test. If we select a volatile attitude by becoming hostile, angry, jealous or suspicious, then *we* have failed the test. If we condemn ourselves by believing that we are unworthy, then again, *we* have failed the test.

If we care at all about ourselves, then we must accept full responsibility for our own feelings. We must learn to guard against those feelings that have the capacity to lead our attitude down the wrong path and to strengthen those feelings that can lead us confidently into a better future.

If we want to receive the rewards the future holds in trust for us, then we must exercise the most important choice given to us as members of the human race by maintaining total dominion over our attitude. Our attitude is an asset, a treasure of great value which must be protected accordingly. Beware of the vandals and thieves among us who would injure our positive attitude or seek to steal it away.

Having the right attitude is one of the basics that success requires. The combination of a sound personal philosophy and a positive attitude about ourselves and the world around us gives us an inner strength and a firm resolve that influences all other areas of our existence... including the third piece of the life puzzle that we will now examine.

CHAPTER THREE

ACTIVITY

There is an ancient story known as the Parable of the Talents. According to the story, one day the master of the household gathered his three servants together and announced that he would soon be going away on a long journey. Before leaving he gave each of his servants a certain number of talents. In those days a talent was worth several years' wages to the average laborer, so each talent represented a substantial sum of money. To one servant he gave five talents; to another he gave two; and to the third he gave one talent. He cautioned the servants to look after these talents in his absence and then left.

While the master was gone the servant with the five talents took them to the marketplace and traded with them until he had converted the five into ten. The second servant did the same, trading his two into four. However, the third servant, being a very cautious man, took the one talent that he had been given and buried it in the ground for safekeeping.

After a time the master returned and gathered his three servants together to inquire about what they had done with the talents he had given to them. The first servant explained how he had wisely traded the five talents he had been given and presented his master with the original five plus the five he had earned. The master said to the servant, "Well done!" The second servant came forward and said that he had also traded wisely and presented his master with the original two talents he had been given plus two more. Again the master said, "Well done!" Finally the third servant stepped forward and told his story. "Fearing that I might lose your money, I carefully buried it in the ground." He then proudly presented the master with the one talent he had been given to look after. The master took one look at the single unused talent and said, "Take the one talent from him and give it to the one who now has ten."

Many people are not very happy with the way this story ends. After all, it does not seem *fair* to take the little that the third servant had and give it to the servant who had ten. But remember, life is not designed to give rewards in proportion to our level of *need*, it gives them in proportion to our level of *deserve*. The moral of this story is that whatever life has handed to us, whether it is one talent or a hundred, it is our responsibility to do something with what we have been given! That is how we change pennies into fortunes and obstacles into opportunity - by taking all that we have and all that we are and putting it to work.

Sooner or later we must convert knowledge and good feelings into activity. And as the parable also clearly demonstrates, the more we start with, the more we will receive for all of our disciplined work. That is why starting with a sound personal philosophy and the right attitude is so important. The more we know and the better we feel about ourselves and our opportunities, the greater our chances for success will be.

But a growing awareness and a positive attitude are not enough in and of themselves. What we know and how we feel merely determine our *potential* for achievement. Whether we actually achieve our goals is ultimately determined by our *activity*.

We can have a well-balanced philosophy, great depth of character, and a good attitude about life, but unless we put these valuable assets to work, we may find ourselves making more excuses than progress. What we know and how we feel are important factors that affect the quality of our lives. But remember, they are merely the foundation upon which to build a better future. Completing the rest of the picture requires *action*.

Why We Sometimes Get Stuck On The Ground Floor

If we have a sincere desire for progress, then we are compelled to find every possible means to implement all that we know and feel. We must find ways to demonstrate on the *outside* all of the value that we possess on the *inside*. Otherwise, our values will remain unappreciated and our talents unrewarded.

Why some people fail and others succeed can be baffling. Sometimes it may even seem *unfair*. We all know people who have a good education, the right attitude and a sincere desire to make something of themselves. They are good parents, honest employees and loyal friends. Yet despite their knowledge, feelings and desires, they continue to lead lives of quiet desperation. They should *have* so much more than they do, but they seem to receive so little.

Then there are those who always seem to receive so much and yet merit so little. They have no education. They have a poor attitude about themselves and other people, and are often dishonest and unethical. The only thing they

seem to share in common with those who *should* do well
but do so poorly is a sincere desire to get ahead. Despite
their lack of virtues, knowledge and appreciation, these
people often seem to come out on top.

Why is it that some good people seem to have so little
while the dishonest seem to have so much? Why is it that
the drug dealers and the mob members and the criminal
element in our society are driving Rolls Royces while many
are struggling to make the payments on their inexpensive
compacts? If our desire to succeed is as strong as theirs,
and if we have the added virtues of philosophical refinement and emotional sophistication, why are we not all
doing better than they are?

The answer might well be that we do not *work* at
achieving our goals...and they *do*. We do not take all that
we *are* to the marketplace and put it to work. They *do*. We
do not stay up late at night developing new plans to achieve
our dreams and work hard day after day to make those
dreams a reality. They *do*. We do not learn all that we
possibly can about our industry and our markets. They *do*.
We do not make every effort to get around the right sources
of influence, to associate with those people who can help
us to achieve our goals. They *do*. While we are *dreaming*
about the promise of the future, they are *doing* something
about it. Granted, they may be doing the wrong things, but
they are doing it consistently and with an intensity and a
level of commitment that would put many of us to shame.

Evil always rushes in to fill the void created by the
absence of good. The only thing that is necessry for the
triumph of evil is for good people to do nothing, and
unfortunately, that is what too many good people choose
to do. It is our lack of intense, disciplined activity that has
allowed evil to flourish and good men to flounder. If life
does not seem *fair* sometimes, we have no one to blame
but ourselves.

Imagine how different our world would be if we made a

commitment right now to put into action all that we currently are, *wherever* we currently are, and with *whatever* we currently have. What if we all gave 100 percent to our jobs, our families and our communities? What if, starting right now, we began to read the books, replace errors with disciplines and associate with people who have stimulating ideas? What if, starting right now, we converted our dreams into plans and our plans into refined activities that would lead toward the achievement of our goals? What an incredible difference we could make! In no time at all we would have evil on the run and good would be rushing in to recapture its rightful place. What a life we could then share with our families – a life filled with challenge, excitement and achievement. And what an inheritance we could leave to the next generation – a wealth of virtue, integrity and substance with which to build a whole new world – and all because we cared enough to *do* something with our lives and to put our skills and talents to work.

Harnessing The Vision Of The Future

Niagara Falls is one of the most breathtaking spectacles in the world. Every hour thousands of tons of water flow along the Niagara River and cascade down several hundred feet of rock into the churning, raging waters below. Through man's ingenuity the powerful force of this falling water has been harnessed and now provides an important energy source to hundreds of thousands of people.

Our own dreams can be as breathtaking and powerful as this wonder of nature. But they must also be harnessed and converted into some form of energy if they are to have any value to ourselves and to the world around us. Otherwise, they will remain only an exciting but untapped spectacle of the human imagination.

We all say that we want to succeed, but sooner or later our level of activity must equal our level of intent. *Talking* about achievement is one thing; making it happen is something altogether different.

Some people seem to take more joy in *talking* about success than they do in *achieving* it. It is as though their ritualistic chant about *someday* lulls them into a false sense of security, and all the things that they *should* be doing and *could* be doing on any given day never seem to get done.

The consequences of this self-delusion have their own inevitable price. Sooner or later the day will arrive when they will look back with regret at all those things they could have done, and *meant* to do, but left undone. That is why we must push ourselves in the present to experience the milder pain of discipline. We will all experience one pain or the other – the pain of discipline or the pain of regret – but the difference is that the pain of discipline weighs only ounces while the pain of regret weighs *tons*.

Activity. The application of all that we know and all that we feel, combined with our desire to have more than we have and become more than we are.

Enterprise Is Better Than Ease

If we are involved in a project, how hard *should* we work at it? How much time *should* we put in?

Our philosophy about activity and our attitude about hard work will affect the quality of our lives. What we *decide* about the rightful ratio of labor to rest will establish a certain work ethic. That work ethic – our attitude about the amount of labor we are willing to commit to future fortune – will determine how substantial or how meager that fortune turns out to be.

Enterprise is always better than ease. Every time we choose to do less than we could, this error in judgement has an effect on our self-confidence. Repeated every day, we soon find ourselves not only *doing* less than we should, but also *being* less than we could. The accumulative effect of this error in judgement can be devastating.

Fortunately, it is easy to reverse the process. Any day we choose we can develop a new discipline of *doing* rather than *neglecting*. Every time we choose action over ease or labor over rest, we develop an increasing level of self-worth, self-respect and self-confidence. In the final analysis, it is how we *feel* about ourselves that provides the greatest reward from any activity. It is not what we *get* that makes us valuable, it is what we *become* in the process of *doing* that brings value into our lives. It is activity that converts human dreams into human reality, and that conversion from *idea* into *actuality* gives us a personal value that can come from no other source.

Everything has its price and everything has its pain, but the price and the pain become easy when the promise becomes strong. For the *means* to be filled by intense activity, we must be obsessed by the *ends* – by the promise of the future. The ends will not merely "justify" the means, the inspiration we get from *seeing* the ends clearly in our minds will enable us to *produce* the means.

The Ratio Of Activity To Rest

Life cannot be a process of all work and no rest. It is important to set aside sufficient time to regain our strength. The key is to develop a reasonable ratio of rest to activity.

The Bible offers this philosophy about the ratio of labor to rest: six days of labor and one day of rest. For some this may seem somewhat heavy on the labor side. In fact, there is a new chorus of voices in our country who are at odds with our *current* ratio of five days labor and two days rest. They would have us trim back even further on the labor side and increase the rest period to at least *three* days.

Each of us must select the ratio that best reflects the reward we seek remembering that with diminished labor comes diminished rewards. If we rest too long, the weeds will surely take over the garden. The erosion of our values begins immediately whenever we are at rest. That is why we must make rest a *necessity*, not an *objective*. Rest should only be a necessary pause in the process of preparing for an assault on the next objective and the next discipline.

The punishment for excessive rest is mediocrity.

The Danger In Seeking Short-Cuts To Success

Some of our friends would have us believe that positive affirmation is more important than activity. Rather than doing something constructive to change our lives they would have us repeating various slogans to ourselves that affirm that all is well, such as "Every day and in every way, I am getting better and better."

We must remember that *discipline* is a requirement for progress, and that affirmations *without* discipline is the beginning of delusion.

There is nothing wrong with affirmations provided we remember two important rules. First, we should never allow affirmation to replace action. *Feeling* better is no substitute for *doing* better. And second, whatever we affirm must be the *truth*.

If the truth of our circumstances is that we are broke, then the best affirmation would be to say, "I am broke." That would start the thinking process. Spoken with conviction, these words would drive any reasonably prudent person from ease into action.

If those whose lives are spinning out of control would confront the harsh reality of the truth, and then discipline themselves to *express* that truth rather than disguising it in false and misleading pronouncements, positive change would inevitably result.

72

Reality is always the best beginning. Within reality is the possibility of our own personal miracle. The power of *faith* starts with reality. If we can bring ourselves to state the truth about ourselves and our circumstances, then the truth *will* set us free. Once we finally understand and accept the *truth*, the promise of the future is then freed from the shackles of deception which held it in bondage.

Sooner or later we must stop blaming the government, the pay schedule, the banks, the taxes, our neighbors, the boss, company policy, high prices, our co-workers, our past, our parents, the traffic or the weather for our failure to capture our share of the joy that comes from progress. Once we come to understand how we *really* got to be where and how we are – that the *subtleties* of our repeated and accumulated errors are responsible – then the embarrassment of *that* final truth and our willingness to admit it will start the process of going from pennies to fortune.

Change Begins With Choice

Any day we wish we can discipline ourselves to change it all. Any day we wish we can open the book that will open our mind to new knowledge. Any day we wish we can start a new activity. Any day we wish we can start the process of life change. We can do it immediately, or next week, or next month, or next year.

We can also do nothing. We can pretend rather than perform. And if the idea of having to change ourselves makes us uncomfortable, we can remain as we are. We can choose rest over labor, entertainment over education, delusion over truth, and doubt over confidence. The choices are ours to make. But while we curse the *effect*, we continue to nourish the cause. As Shakespeare uniquely observed, "The fault...is not in the stars, but in *ourselves*."

We *created* our circumstances by our past choices. We have both the ability and the responsibility to make better choices beginning today. Those who are in search of the good life do not need more answers or more time to think things over to reach better conclusions. They need the *truth*. They need the *whole* truth. And they need nothing but the truth.

We cannot allow our errors in judgement, repeated every day, to lead us down the wrong path. We must keep coming back to those basics that make the biggest difference in how our life works out. *Activity* is one of those important basics that we cannot afford to neglect.

The Need For Intelligent Activity

Many of those in search of success and happiness are already working hard, but they just do not seem to be getting anywhere. The problem is that in order to produce the desired results we must put *intelligence* as well as intensity into our activity. Action without intelligence can be destructive. But we must not spend *too much* time in the process of acquiring intelligence. All things must be in their rightful ratio.

It is so easy to mistake motion for progress and movement for achievement. That is why activity must be deliberately planned, carefully refined and consistently executed.

Activity Must Be Planned

We must become wise enough to use today to plan tomorrow. We must *design* the future, not just dream about it. If we discipline ourselves to put intelligence into our plans, we will put fortune into our future.

Our journey toward success cannot be like a Sunday drive. We need to select a specific destination. We also need to anticipate the obstacles and the risks, and be prepared to respond to them whenever they appear.

Having well-defined goals is an essential part of any life plan. These goals should be recorded in writing, and should reflect both short-term and long-range planning. Short-term goals serve as landmarks along the journey. They are the small stepping stones that lead to the achievement of our long-term fortune and help us to stay on track over a long period of time.

Long-range goals serve as milestones. They are the points of achievement along the way that give us cause to celebrate the fruits of our efforts.

But the most important part of planning and goal-setting is to see in our "mind's eye" the major objective that we are pursuing. This is the "magnificent obsession" that we discussed earlier. This is the very nerve center of our ambition. This is what drives us.

Major objectives are the unseen force that pulls us into the future. Through our daily activity and discipline we provide the *push* to propel us toward success. But it is the dream of the future achievement of our objectives that *pulls* us along day after day and pulls us *through* the major obstacles we encounter along the way. The exciting thing about this process is that the more we push, the more the future begins to pull. As we demonstrate our unwaivering determination to conquer our limitations, increase our intelligence and achieve our objective, that still, small voice within us begins to speak its special and promising message *adding* to the pull of the future. As we listen carefully to this voice, and respond instinctively to its urgings, the pull becomes stronger and the future more certain.

A Good Plan Is A Simple Plan

Our better future begins with a worthy objective and a simple plan. We must not allow our plan to become excessively burdened by complexities. Many of the answers take time to discover. It is virtually impossible to plan every detail or to anticipate every obstacle.

We must also be careful not to allow the opinions of others to unduly influence the development of our plan for the good life. Others will have dozens of opinions about what we should do, but the final plan for progress must be *our* plan. We should listen to the voices of value, but we must remember that no one else will see our plan or sense our obsession quite the way we do. It must be a personally designed plan, and its creator and architect must remain at the helm of the ship throughout the entirety of the journey.

Activity Must Be Disciplined

Discipline. A word that we have used repeatedly throughout this book, and for very good reason. There is a tendency for the negative side of life to infiltrate our plans, our dreams and our activities in an effort to seize control. There is a tendency for optimism to surrender to doubt. There is a tendency for a simple plan to become a *complex* plan. There is a tendency for courage to give way to fear, and for confidence to be overwhelmed by worry.

Only through the consistent application of discipline can we prevent the negative tendencies of life from destroying our plans. With the passing of a little time and the attainment of a little success, we can become careless. That is why those in pursuit of the good life must develop a new sense of appreciation for discipline, and become aware of all that they can do and all that they can have.

What each of us *can* do is remarkable. People can do the most amazing things, once they have made the decision to tackle the disciplines that lead to a new philosophy, a new attitude, and a new and intense level of activity. What people *will* do, however, is sometimes disappointing.

Any day we choose we can walk away from wherever we are *regardless* of the circumstances. "Apple by apple," one page at a time, one paragraph at a time, one new discipline at a time, we can begin the process of amending our activity to such a degree that *today* can become the starting point of a whole new life.

Anyone can do it!

We do it by designing a good plan. We do it by setting new goals. We do it by working every day on the little things that will make a major difference in how our lives turn out. Like everything else that success requires, developing the discipline that it takes to achieve our dreams is easy to do...*and* it is also easy not to do.

The Starting Point Of Disciplined Activity

Here is one of the best places to start on the process of working on new disciplines. Everyone has a mental list of "I should have's"—

"I should have written to my mother this weekend."

"I should have told her how much I really care long before now."

"I should have called that creditor and told the truth last month."

"I should have started my exercise program years ago."

Any day we choose we can go to work on the basics—on any one of a host of small activities that will start the process of self-discipline. The joy that comes from this small achievement will start the miracle process.

The *early* inspiration that comes from the practice of new and simple disciplines will start a process called "soaring self-worth." It does not matter how small or how insignificant the activity is because it is within those obscure but important disciplines that the great opportunities exist.

This kind of simple progress will build a ladder leading out of the abyss of failure and neglect that once was our dwelling place. With each new discipline we will have constructed a new rung that will enable us to climb out of the darkness where the failures, the complainers, and the confused and misguided gather to share their sad stories of how unfair life is.

Building the ladder is *easy* to do, but it is also easy *not* to do.

The smallest of disciplines, practiced every day, start an incredible process that can change our lives forever.

Until we have learned to take care of the little opportunities life brings our way, we will never master the disciplines for becoming happy and prosperous. The *major* accomplishments in life begin with the mastery of the *small* disciplines. The mental, emotional and philosophical "muscles" required to write a letter, clean the garage or pay our bills on time are the very same "muscles" involved in running a company or managing a department. As a wise prophet has written:

> "Be not weary in well-doing, for
> in due season you shall reap if
> you faint not."

We cannot rule the city until we can rule our spirit.

We cannot rule the nation until we can rule *ourselves*.

We cannot design our future until we have redesigned our habits.

We cannot increase our rewards until we increase our level of intelligent activity.

ACTIVITY

The place to start is within ourselves through the development of new disciplines. That is where success *really* starts, by becoming the master over the *small* details of our lives. All of the great rewards in life are available to each of us, if we will discipline ourselves to walk through those early stages of growth without neglecting any of the disciplines. We must not permit any small activity to rob us of our future health and wealth and friendship and lifestyle. We cannot allow any error in judgement to delude us into thinking that "letting the little things slide" would not make a major difference. We cannot say to ourselves — "This is the only area where I am letting down on my self-discipline." It is this "only area" that will start the process of erosion on all of our other disciplines.

One of the great challenges facing us all is disciplined activity. We must discipline the reach of our knowledge, for we can have too much as well as too little. We must discipline ourselves to maintain a proper attitude, for we are surrounded by sources that can quickly erode the attitude we have worked so hard to develop. And we must discipline ourselves to convert dreams into plans, and plans into goals, and goals into those small daily activities that will lead us, one sure step at a time, toward a better future.

Finally, we must use the power of our imagination. We must ponder all that is possible. We must remind ourselves that to do what is *possible* we must sometimes challenge ourselves with the *impossible*. As an ancient warrior once wrote, "It is better to aim the spear at the moon and strike the eagle, than to aim at the eagle and strike only a rock."

Planning, imagination and intense activity are awesome forces that have the power to dramatically change the quality of our lives.

Activity is a major part of the life puzzle. It is the power that gives substance and meaning to our philosophy and our attitude. Intelligent, planned, intense, and consistent activity creates new energy and keeps us moving toward the exciting future that our thoughts and desires have already designed for us.

CHAPTER FOUR

RESULTS

Any business or personal *activity* undertaken in the proper season, and combined with the passage of enough time, will produce a predictable *result*. The reason for the seasons is *productivity*, and the purpose of our activity is *results*.

Results are the harvest that comes from our past efforts. If the farmer has planted only a handful of seeds in the spring, he cannot expect to reap a very bountiful harvest in the fall. Likewise, if a person has engaged in only minimal activity in the *past*, he should not expect significant results in the *present*.

Results are always in direct proportion to effort. Those who rest in the spring do not reap in the fall, regardless of need and regardless of desire. Results are the reward reserved for those who had the foresight to seize an earlier opportunity. If the opportunity was missed, the reward will be withheld.

The opportunity of springtime is brief. Opportunity

approaches, arrives and then quickly passes. It does not linger; nor does it pause to look back. Opportunity merely presents itself, and those who respond to its arrival with intelligent *activity* will realize a full measure of the desired *result*.

All that we do determines our future results. Like the farmer who tills the soil in preparation for planting the seed, we must work to develop a sound philosophy. Like the farmer who cultivates and fertilizes his crop to destroy the weeds and nourish the growing seeds, we must strive to develop a new attitude. And like the farmer who tends his crop from morning until nightfall in anticipation of the future harvest, we must engage in labor – in daily activity.

If our past labors have produced a poor harvest, there is nothing we can do about it. We cannot alter the past. We cannot ask nature to make an exception to the rules no matter how hungry we are. Nor will nature permit us to ask the soil for an advance. The only thing we can do is to prepare for the inevitable arrival of another spring – another opportunity – and then plant, nourish and tend our new crop as diligently as possible, remembering the painful consequences of our past neglect. In *remembering* the consequences, however, we must not allow ourselves to be *overcome* by them. Their lessons must *serve* us, not *overwhelm* us.

Throughout our lives we will experience a number of springtimes and a number of harvests. Our future happiness is seldom the product of any one harvest. Rather, it is the result of scores of individual opportunities which are either well-used or sadly neglected. For our happiness lies in the accumulative effect of our past activity. This is why it is so important to study results. Checking our results on a regular basis provides us with an excellent indicator of how well we are using our opportunities. Our current results are an early indicator of what the future will likely hold in store as we continue along our present course. If our current results are satisfying, then the future will likely produce the same bountiful harvest. If our current results are not as we would like them to be, then we need to take a closer look at those factors that may have nudged or even pushed us in the wrong direction.

How To Measure Our Results

The results of our past efforts can be measured in several different ways. The first way to measure our results is by looking at what we *have*. Our homes, cars, bank accounts, investments, and all of our other tangible assets are a good measuring rod of our material progress.

Our *assets* reflect one aspect of our current *value*. To measure our value, we merely examine our *assets*. Now this is not to suggest that the only way to measure value is by a list of our material possessions. There are all kinds of wealth, and the greatest fortunes in life – joy, health, love, family, experiences, friendships – will always outweigh the value of any material possessions we might acquire. But what we have accumulated over the years in the form of material assets can be a good indicator of past efforts and possible *future* results.

If we currently have a significant accumulation of money and material possessions, we are probably well on our way toward achieving that dream known as *financial independence*. By the same token, if our list of assets is rather meager despite our efforts over the last ten, twenty or thirty years of labor, then this may be a good indicator that *something* needs to *change*. We may need to make some major changes in our current level of *activity* in order to increase our results. We may need to increase our skills or our knowledge or our awareness in order to take better advantage of life's opportunities. Or we may need to make a few adjustments to our *philosophy* about money and to our *attitude* about spending.

If we are not satisfied with what we have achieved at this point in our lives, then *now* is the time to fix the future. Unless we change how we *are* right now, what we *have* will always be about the same. The same seed sown by the same sower will inevitably produce the same harvest.

For the *harvest* to change, it may be necessary to change the seed, the soil, or more likely than not, the *sower*. Perhaps the sower insists on using a plan that simply cannot work. It may be that the sower believes that sowing should be done in the summer instead of the spring. When winter arrives and the sower's need is great, he or she may be found standing in the barren field condemning circumstances for the failure of the soil to yield its promised harvest. This would be the ideal time for the misguided sower to *measure* – to assess the reasons why the soil did not cooperate with an ill-conceived plan. But instead of measuring and assessing, the sower complains and compiles yet another list of reasons for his or her unfortunate dilemma.

Everything we have acquired is a result of past efforts and past thoughts. We gather intelligence or we gather ingnorance, and our future will produce rewards commensurate with what we have done with the past. We must use our time to plan, to labor, to measure, to invest, to share, to refine past activity, and to add to our storehouse of knowledge. These are the seeds we must gather along the way so that the quality of our results will improve with each passing year.

Another important way to measure our results is to take a closer look at what we have *become*. What sort of people have we attracted into our lives? Are we well-respected by our co-workers and neighbors? Do we honor our beliefs? Do we try to see someone else's point of view? Are we listening to our children? Do we express sincere appreciation to our parents, our spouses and our friends? Are we honest and ethical in our business transactions?

Are we known for our unwaivering integrity among our peers? Do we still march to the beat of a different drummer? Are we happy with who and what we have become?

What we have become is a result of all of our past experiences and how we have handled them. What we have become is also a result of the personal changes we have either voluntarily or involuntarily made over the years. If we are not happy with what we have become, then we must change what we *are*. For things to change, *we* must change... that is one of life's fundamentals.

We Attract What We Have By The Person We Have Become

In designing a better future the major focus of our plan should be on becoming more than we already are. If we are not happy with our current results, then the place to begin is with *ourselves*.

Everything we have in life – the tangibles as well as the intangibles – is a direct result of who we are. The answer to the good life lies in becoming more than we currently are so that we can attract more than we currently have.

If we lost everything tomorrow, we could easily replace it all. Why? Because we acquired those things as a result of what we are. Assuming "what we are" has not changed, in time we will attract back into our lives everything we may have lost. The same applied knowledge, the same attitude, the same effort and the same plan will always produce the same results.

This fundamental should give us cause for both elation and alarm. The elation comes from the fact that any day we choose, we can begin to make changes within ourselves that will attract even more good things into our lives. The alarm comes from the fact that unless we *make* those necessary changes, unless we convert our errors into new disciplines, and our dreams into well-defined plans and intelligent, consistent activity, we will always have exactly what we now have. We will always live in the same home, drive the same car, know the same friends and experience the same frustrations and set-backs that we have *always* experienced because *we* have not changed. The results will always be predictable because results are always determined by what we are in the process of becoming.

Doing *more* is only part of the answer. The real answer lies in becoming more than we are so that our increased potential becomes an integral part of everything we do. That is how life gets better – when *we* get better. We cannot have more without first becoming more. That is one of the basics.

Success Must Be Attracted, Not Pursued

Personal value is the magnet that attracts all good things into our lives. The greater our value, the greater our reward. Since the solution for *having* more is *becoming* more, we must be in constant search for new ways to increase our *value*. Self-control, the practice of discipline, patience, planning, intensity of effort, the wise investment of a good portion of our results, the development of a well-balanced attitude, consistent activity, the gathering of knowledge, frequent reading and a sensible personal philosophy are all examples of ways in which our value can be increased.

It is the acquisition of more *value* that we must pursue, not more valuables. Our objective must be to work harder on *ourselves* than we work on anything else. By giving careful attention to our philosophy, our attitude and our activity, we are making a positive contribution to what we are *becoming*, and in the process of becoming more than we now are, we will attract more than we now have.

86

Better Results Come From Being A Better Person

We *become* and then we *attract.* We grow personally and then we advance materially. Unfortunately, the vast majority seems to have the plan reversed. Their philosophy is "If I had more money, I would be a better person." But that's not the way life is designed to work. *Having* more doesn't make us more. It merely magnifies what we already are. Those who cannot save a few pennies out of meager earnings will never be able to save dollars out of future fortunes. The same discipline it takes to put a few coins in a jar every week is the same discipline it takes to open a savings account or manage an investment portfolio.

Conversation about our intended progress will only take us so far and promises about the future will only buy us a little time. Promises must soon be matched by *performance.* If the results do not appear in a reasonable amount of time, we run the risk of losing the trust of others in addition to our own self-respect. We may find that those who once believed no longer believe, and we will one day be left only with our well-intentioned, but unfulfilled pronouncements.

A loss of this magnitude is worth preventing. It is on the day when we discover our losses that we will taste the bitter pill of neglect. It is on *that* day when we will finally experience the agonizing consequences of self-delusion, procrastination and unkept promises.

Will we read the books, make the plans, make good use of time, invest a portion of all that we earn, polish our current skills, attend classes to develop new skills, and get around better people in order to improve our chances for success? Will we tell the truth, improve our ability to communicate, use our journals, and give careful attention to all the virtues that success requires? Or will we be content to let the time slip through our fingers like grains of sand while we slowly lose self-confidence, the respect of others, and perhaps even the few possessions and valuable relationships that our past efforts have managed to attract into our lives? Will we go on sitting idly by while our dreams diminish to memories, as hope gives way to remorse?

Surely not.

The Future Rewards Are Always There Waiting For Us

As certainly as we *once* dreamed, we can dream again. As surely as we once believed, we can believe again. No matter where we are right now, we *still* have the ability to change it all.

The journey toward success is a journey of a thousand steps, and it begins with a single book or a single promise finally kept. It begins with the awakening of our sleeping spirit brought on by dreams of all that *could* be.

Any day we choose we can stand up and take that first step on a journey that can lead us to a new and better way of life. We must not expect the results merely because we have begun the activity, but with continued effort and certain steps will surely come our future rewards.

The Value Of New Skills

The development of new skills is vitally important if we expect to make major progress and improve the level of our performance. A person can chop down a tree with a hammer, but it might take thirty days. By learning to use an axe he can accomplish the same goal in thirty minutes.

Life and labor get easier when knowledge is combined with new skills. Skill is the *refinement* of our current abilities added to the *acquisition* of new talents. It is the result of investigation driven by curiosity. It is the result of creativity and imagination intelligently applied to new methods. It is a product of refined attempts as emerging quality rises to new levels. Skill is also a thorough understanding of the task at hand that comes from patient study and serious observation.

Skill is what is acquired when a person becomes the master of a task. It is having full confidence in our ability and in our command of the many intricacies of our jobs. Skill is the process of learning. Skill is the result of accumulating a mountain of experience and the never-ending dedication to making good things better.

Those who would possess happiness and success must first master as many skills as they can gather up, blending each into all of the rest until finally a unique talent emerges. With the accumulated value of our skills and talents, all things become possible.

The First Step For Getting Better Results

How dramatically we can change our results is largely a function of imagination. In 1960, it was a technological impossibility for man to travel into outer space. Within ten years, however, the first man stepped out onto the surface of the moon. The miraculous process of converting the dream into reality began when one voice challenged the scientific community to do whatever was necessary to see to it that America "places a man on the moon by the end of this decade." That challenge awakened the spirit of a nation by planting the seed of possible future achievement into the fertile soil of imagination. With that one bold challenge the impossible became a reality.

Can a poor person become wealthy? Of course! The unique combination of desire, planning, effort and perseverance will always work its magic. The question is not whether the *formula* for success will work, but rather whether the person will work the formula. That is the

89

unknown variable. That is the challenge that confronts us all. We can all go from wherever we are to wherever we want to be. No dream is impossible provided we first have the courage to believe in it.

If We Will Pay The Price, We Will Inherit The Promise

Solving financial difficulty is *easy*. But it is also easy *not* to solve. If the rewards are eluding us, then the best place to start is with an honest look at our results.

If the results are not there, something is *wrong*. The lack of results is *symptomatic* of a problem that needs to be addressed and corrected. To ignore the symptom is merely to perpetuate the cause. Rarely will a problem repair itself. Instead, a neglected problem *intensifies*.

Those whose efforts have produced a poor result often have a lengthy list of reasons to justify their poor progress. To them the items on the list are not excuses, they are *reasons*. They blame the company or they blame the boss. They blame taxes. They blame their parents or the teachers or the system. Sometimes they even blame the *country*.

But there is nothing wrong with the country. Eastern Europe has recently battered down the walls just to get a taste of the opportunities enjoyed by those laboring under the banner of capitalism. They will gladly confront the challenges because they have hungered so long for its rewards. Their industries will soon be competing with our own to produce new products, bring better service, and introduce new technologies with which to create new results and new rewards for themselves.

There is no shortage of opportunity in America. There is only a shortage of those who will apply themselves to the basics that success requires.

Check Results Often

We cannot afford to wait ten years to see if our plan, our philosophy, our attitude or our efforts need to be modified. Neglect and delay can be costly.

Progress must be measured on a regular basis. The timely checking of the key indicators in all parts of our lives is a barometer of responsible thinking. How often we need to check our results depends on how far we want to go. The greater the distance, the more frequently we need to check. If we are only going as far as the next block, being off a few degrees isn't going to make much difference. But if we have our sights set on some distant star, then miscalculating by even one degree can lead us millions of miles off target. The longer we wait to discover this small error in judgement, the harder we will have to work to get back on course. And of greater consequence is that the passage of time tends to diminish our desire to get back on course. We may accept the little that we have and abandon our dreams of all that we might have been.

Making Measurable Progress In A Reasonable Amount Of Time

That is the great challenge of life – making measurable progress in a reasonable amount of time. That is what creates both purpose and value in our lives.

If we are to confront this challenge with enthusiasm and with any hope for success, we cannot use our current circumstances as an excuse for our failure to make measureable progress. When circumstances make progress difficult, this should be our signal to push harder, not to diminish our efforts.

The difficulties we encounter serve a unique *purpose*. Difficulty tests the strength of our resolve. If our *want* to is strong enough, then we will be driven to seek solutions. As

91

we invoke the power of creativity and intensify our efforts to conquer each new problem, we actually speed up our progress.

Without challenges to capture our attention we may take twice as long to arrive at our objective. If the way is easy, we tend to drift along at a leisurely pace, content in the knowledge that success is within our grasp. If the way is fraught with obstacles, we will dig deeper within ourselves calling upon more ingenuity, more abilities and more strength than we even knew we possessed. Conquering these challenges leads to a new level of self-confidence that drives us further and faster toward our inevitable success.

If we are not making measurable progress in a reasonable amount of time, then it may be that our goals are too small. It is difficult to get excited about minor rewards.

The problem may also be that we really do not believe in our dreams, or to be more specific, believe in our ability to make them happen. Instead of being challenged by obstacles, we use them as opportunities to withdraw from the confrontation. That is why checking our results often is so important. If we are not making measureable progress in a reasonable amount of time, then something is clearly wrong with either our objectives or the execution of our plans.

Whatever Happens, Happens To Us All

In the final analysis, we are all faced with about the same circumstances over the period of a lifetime. Some choose to use them as an excuse for poor performance while others use those same circumstances as a reason to grow and to drive themselves to new heights of accomplishment.

We all have opportunity mixed with difficulty. All of us have times of illness in addition to years of health. The storms come upon the rich as well as the poor.

Whatever happens, happens to us all. The only difference is our approach to the "things that happen." It is not what happens that determines the quality of our lives, it is what we choose to *do* about what happens.

There is an inherent tendency to want the results when we *want* them or *need* them. But the law of sowing and reaping tells us that to reap in the fall we must first plant in the spring. We must use the summer to help the plants to grow strong by guarding against the certain invasion of the devouring insects and the strangling weeds. We must continue our *activity* in spite of our current needs. The harvest will surely come, but it will come in its own due season:

"To every thing there is a season, and to every purpose under the heaven: A time to be born and a time to die; a time to plant and a time to pluck up that which is planted; ...A time to weep and a time to laugh; a time to mourn and a time to dance. ...A time to love and a time to hate; a time of war and a time of peace."

Results do not respond to need. Results respond to effort...to labor...to *activity*. If we have done our part, the results we need *will* appear in a reasonable amount of time.

Neglect Intensifies Future Challenges

While challenges can serve a worthwhile function in helping us to achieve our goals, there is no need to deliberately invite them into our lives.

Ten years from now we will all be *somewhere*, the question is *where*? *Now* is the time to fix the next ten years. Life will present us with enough obstacles without purposely attracting them to us.

One of the best ways to minimize future challenges is

to anticipate the results of our current neglect. Anticipating the results of our current neglects begins with asking ourselves important questions about our attention to the basics:

How many books have I read in the past ninety days?

How regularly did I exercise last month?

How much of my income have I invested this past year?

How many letters have I written in the past week?

How many times have I written in my journal this month?

The answers to these and many other questions will provide us with vital information about our potential for progress and future rewards. If we cannot discipline ourselves in the small things, we will lack the discipline to capitalize on the great opportunities when they appear.

Every error defeated by disciplined activity paves the way for our future success. And *that* is how the life puzzle is completed – a single victory at a time.

The Value of Confidence In Determining Results

Those who pursue the good life should never settle for less than the best they can be. Doing less than our best has a disastrous effect. It erodes self-confidence and diminishes our self-worth.

Doing less than we can inevitably affects our attitude. It leads to a bottomless pit of degrading emotions, and produces embarassing and discouraging results.

Doing less than we can creates guilt; guilt leads to worry, and worry gives birth to self-doubt. Then comes the inevitable loss of self-confidence and the blueprint for failure is now virtually complete. The less capable we feel, the less we do, and less activity means fewer results. As our results decline, so does our attitude. The negative spiral has now begun and our lives are soon spinning out of control.

And how did it all begin? When we allowed ourselves to do *less* than we *could* have done. The growing weight of things left undone undermines our confidence not only in ourselves, but also in the possibility of a better future.

But there is a solution for those whose lives are caught up in this negative spiral. By going to work on our *attitude*, we put ourselves in a better position to begin the process of taking *action*. From increased activity we can produce new results. From these early results our self-confidence will once again begin to grow. And as our confidence increases we push ourselves into new activities which produce new results, and that improves our attitude even more. Suddenly, what was once a life spinning out of control is a life headed toward the pull of the future. It begins with doing whatever is necessary to change our *attitude* – the beginning point of all human progress and achievement.

Sometimes the best prescription for a poor attitude is *activity*. We may find ourselves with an acceptable attitude, and needing only *involvement* in which to apply our talent. It has been wisely said, "Weak is he that permits his attitude to control his actions, and strong is he who *forces* his actions to control his thoughts." Whether the recipe for success begins with activity or attitude, the essential step is to go to work on one or the other. It is *inactivity*, regardless of the cause, that is unacceptable.

Action can begin with writing a long-overdue letter or making an important, but difficult telephone call. It can be the purchase of a journal or the reading of a book. It can be the simple act of turning off the radio and turning on a cassette tape that will provide new insights.

Whenever our lives are turned upside down, we have

only to find something worth doing to change things for the better. We must do it with waivering confidence in the beginning. We may have to do it *despite* the presence of fear. But inevitably, our doubts and fears will step aside when our unyielding commitment to take action comes into the picture. The results produced by these initial acts of faith will become the foundation upon which to build a whole new life.

Results are more than just an objective; they are the seeds of future joy and prosperity. Every result we experience, no matter how small, is another certain step taken toward a life of achievement.

How Far Should We Reach?

It seems that every life form on this planet strives toward its *maximum* potential...except human beings.

A tree does not grow to half its potential size and then say, "I guess that will do." A tree will drive its roots as deep as possible. It will soak up as much nourishment as it can, stretch as high and as wide as nature will allow, and then look down as if to remind us of how much each of *us* could *become* if we would only do all that we can.

Why is it that human beings, surely the most intelligent life form on earth, do not strive to achieve their maximum potential? Why is it that we allow ourselves to stop half way? Why are we not constantly striving to become all that we can be? The reason is simple: We have been given the freedom of choice.

In most cases choice is a gift. But when it comes to *doing* all that we can with our abilities and our opportunities, choice can sometimes be more of a curse than a blessing. All too often we choose to do far less than we *could* do. We would rather relax under the shade of the growing tree than to emulate its struggle for greatness.

The Two Choices We Face

Each of us has two distinct choices to make about what we will do with our lives. The first choice we can make is to be *less* than we have the capacity to be. To earn less. To have less. To read less and think less. To try less and discipline ourselves less. These are the choices that lead to an empty life. These are the choices that, once made, lead to a life of constant *apprehension* instead of a life of wondrous *anticipation*.

And the second choice? To do it all! To become all that we can possibly be. To read every book that we possibly can. To earn as much as we possibly can. To give and share as much as we possibly can. To strive and produce and accomplish as much as we possibly can. All of us have that choice.

To do or *not* to do. To be or *not* to be. To be *all* or to be *less* or to be nothing at all.

Like the tree, it would be a worthy challenge for us all to stretch upward and outward to the full measure of our capabilities. Why not do all that we can, every moment that we can, the best that we can, for as long as we can?

Our ultimate life objective should be to create as much as our talent and ability and desire will permit. To settle for doing less than we could do is to fail in this worthiest of undertakings.

Results are the best measurement of human progress. Not conversation. Not explanation. Not justification. Results! And if our results are less than our potential suggests that they *should* be, then we must strive to become more today than we were the day before. The greatest rewards are always reserved for those who bring great value to themselves and the world around them as a result of who and what they have *become*.

97

CHAPTER FIVE

LIFESTYLE

The final blending of our philosophy, attitude, activity and results is what creates this final personal quest that we call *lifestyle*.

Lifestyle is how we choose to live and how we design our lives. It is the sophisticated understanding of the difference between life's trinkets and life's treasures.

Many have learned to *earn* well, but they have not yet learned to *live* well. It's as though they have decided to wait until they become wealthy before they start practicing sophistication. What they fail to understand is that practiced sophistication is as much a *cause* of wealth as it is a result of wealth.

Some attribute their poor attitude about life to their low level of income. They maintain that if they ever solved their money problems, they would show us what happiness is really all about. Obviously, they have not yet discovered that it was their failure to find happiness in the past that has affected their current income. If they continue with this error in judgement, their lack of happiness in the present will determine their *future* income as well. Until they have discovered that happiness is part of the *cause* and that wealth is merely an *effect*, their circumstances are not likely to change.

Lifestyle Is A Reflection Of Our Attitude And Our Values

As we have already examined, how we feel and what we deem to be worthwhile is part of the *mental* process that ultimately determines what we attract into our lives. If we are not happy with our current circumstances, we can begin to change them simply by changing how we think and feel.

Lifestyle is also a function of this same thinking process. Any day we choose we have the ability to alter our lifestyle by changing how we feel and making better decisions about what we deem to be valuable.

The exciting thing about lifestyle is that we can have it all now! We don't have to wait *until* we are wealthy or powerful or famous to experience happiness. We don't have to postpone our appreciation of the finer things in life *until* we have reached our career goals. We can live a life that is as joyful and rewarding as we might wish starting right now.

Anyone can give money to charity. But the real rewards lie in the giving of ourselves and our time.

For little more that the price of a movie ticket anyone can attend a symphony orchestra. The music is just as stirring from the back of a concert hall during an afternoon matinee as it is from high up in a private box on opening night.

You don't have to *own* a Rembrandt to appreciate his incredible genius.

Given with sincerity, a single, long-stemmed rose can

100

be more meaningful than a dozen orchids.

The price of admission to a fabulous sunset is still free.

We don't have to be rich to live richly. All of the happiness and fulfillment we want can be ours right now simply by changing how we feel and what we think about this concept called lifestyle.

Lifestyle Is Not An Amount

Culture is not an amount. Sophistication is not an amount. And neither is lifestyle. They are arts to be practiced by those who wish for more of the good life. To become the masters of these arts, the practice must begin with what we *currently* have.

Each of us, regardless of our circumstances, can begin the art of practiced sophistication any time we choose. For example, we are all familiar with the process of tipping those who provide us with service in a restaurant. But few of us know the origin and purpose of leaving a tip. The word "tip" is an abbreviation of the phrase "To Insure Promptness." To insure *promptness* implies that the gratuity should be given *before* we receive the service, not after.

The sophisticated approach to dining out is to take aside the person who will be serving us and present the tip in *advance* of the service we seek, not after. Of course, the gratuity should be an amount sufficient to assure that the level of service will be well above average. To add to the uniqueness of the act, we might also combine some rather uncommon words with our unique gesture such as, "My guests tonight are very special and I want to give them the best possible experience. I would like for you to make sure that they are well taken care of, so here is something special for *You*."

This brief moment of conversation, combined with the

small amount of money that would be required, will work wonders. It will be especially effective if the words are spoken with sincerity and accentuated with a warm smile. That is what sophistication is all about – finding simple ways to live uniquely. Anyone can do it. It's easy to do.

It is also easy *not* to do. It is easy to eat the meal, tolerate poor service, become angry and ruin the special occasion by not doing the small, but special things in an extraordinary way.

Lifetyle is really nothing more than the art of doing ordinary things extraordinarily well. It isn't getting up from the meal, and because of the poor service, tossing two quarters on the table and glaring at the waiter on the way out the door. Imagine the effect that such unsophisticated conduct would have on those you had hoped to impress. It would convert a potentially memorable event into a nightmare, and all because of the missed opportunity of taking a brief moment – and investing a few extra dollars – *to insure promptness*.

We must learn to spend small sums in a tasteful manner before we can ever hope to master the art of handling major expenditures with sophistication.

Lifestyle Is A Reflection Of Who And What We Are

Our lifestyle communicates a clear message about who we are and how we *think*. Lifestyle is where we go, what we do, and how we feel once we are there. Lifestyle is how we dress, what we drive, and the type of entertainment we choose to enjoy.

Lifestyle is a mixture of substance as well as style, refinement as well as intellect, and emotional control in times of challenge as well as emotional *release* in times of joy and happiness.

Successful people, and those in serious pursuit of

success, tend to communicate the level of sophistication and intelligence they have managed to acquire. How they conduct themselves leaves little doubt about their intensity for personal development and for personal achievement.

Everything about us is sending a message to others about our level of intensity as well. The things we do, the things we say, even our appearance is *suggestive* of an inner attitude about life. If we are spending more money on donuts than we do on books, that suggests something about the sincerity of our desire for personal progress.

Whether we spend an evening with a book, in front of a computer screen or a tv screen, talking with our children or having fun with our "pals from the office," lifestyle is a function of attitude and personal values. We can all afford to live better. It doesn't take more money to change how we live. It takes more deliberate thought and a greater appreciation of the real values in life.

Lifestyle Is Not An Automatic Reward

Lifestyle means *designing* ways to live uniquely. It is a skill to be mastered, not a condition to be pursued. Lifestyle is finding new ways to bring joy, pleasure, excitement, and substance into our lives and into the lives of those we care for while we are *working* on our goals, not once we have achieved them. A more abundant existence does not necessarily mean a more enjoyable lifestyle.

Many of us dream of becoming wealthy, of having a beautiful home that is tended by others so that we will be free to enjoy ourselves. We dream of winning lotteries that will enable us to quit our jobs tomorrow and go off in pursuit of the good life. We dream of chauffeurs to drive us and servants to take care of us so that we can have all the time in the world to do whatever we want to do.

The big question is what *would* we do? In a very short time, most of what we dreamed of one day doing would become as uninspiring as our current lifestyle. There is only so much traveling, so much partying, so much sleeping, and so much "enjoying" that we can experience before this too would become tedious.

If it is not a life of endless fun and laughter that we are after, then what *is* it that we are in pursuit of? What *is* this thing we call lifestyle?

We may all have different opinions of what lifestyle is, but hopefully we will all agree on what it is not: It is *not* something we *get* simply as a result of having more. Lifestyle is a result of *living* more...living more fully, living more consciously, living more joyfully, living more appreciatively. The more fully we live, the more we do and the more we become. Lifestyle is not a reward for all of our hard effort, it is a way of making our hard effort more rewarding, more meaningful and ultimately more productive.

Lifestyle Must Be Studied As Well As Practiced

If we wish to be wealthy, we must study wealth, and if we wish to be happy, we must study happiness. The combination of these two studies creates the aura that we call lifestyle.

Most people do not make happiness and wealth a *study*. Their plan for finding happiness consists of going through the day with their fingers crossed, hoping that somehow, something will work out that will make them happy. But happiness is an art, not an accident. It is not something that falls out of the sky. Happiness – that unique emotion that we mistakenly believe comes to us only when we have become successful – must *precede* the achievement of success. Happiness is as much a *cause* of success as it is a result of success, and we can begin to experience happiness whenever we wish, regardless of our current circumstances.

104

Learn To Be Happy With What You Have While You Strive For What You Want

Each of us can design our own life happiness. We can *design* it and we can experience it. We do not have to wait. Waiting will merely prolong the agony of putting up with poor service, short tempers, ruined moments of joy, and a continuation of life as it has always been.

That exquisite feeling called happiness can begin wherever and however we are because it has nothing to do with *things*. Having more isn't the answer to happiness. If we can count our blessings on only two or three fingers, then putting diamonds on those same fingers isn't going to give us more blessings. If we have failed to develop meaningful friendships when our resources were meager, then we aren't going to be any better at finding or keeping good friends when our finances improve. The experience of a meaningful relationship with someone who has been with us through the good times and the bad, who knows us and cares about us in a way that makes us feel good just to know that they are in this world, is something we cannot afford to postpone.

There is as much joy in watching our children learn to ride on a secondhand bicycle as watching them wobble away on a new one. Are we going to deny them or ourselves that incredible experience simply because we can't afford the best or the most expensive toys right now?

Happiness isn't something you withdraw from your bank account. It is something to withdraw from life and from those around you. There is nothing wrong with wanting more for ourselves and for our families. But it doesn't mean that we have to experience less of life's treasures because we *have* less or that we will appreciate them more when we *have* more. If we cannot learn to be happy with what we have right now, then we will never be happy no matter how much good fortune comes our way.

Wherever You Are, *BE* There

One of the major reasons why we fail to find happiness or to create a unique lifestyle is because we have not yet mastered the art of *being*.

While we are home our thoughts are still absorbed with solving the challenges we face at the office. And when we are at the office we find ourselves worrying about problems at home.

We go through the day without really listening to what others are saying to us. We may be hearing the words, but we aren't absorbing the message.

As we go through the day we find ourselves focusing on past experiences or future possibilities. We are so involved in yesterday and tomorrow that we never even notice that today is slipping by.

We go *through* the day rather than getting something *from* the day. We are everywhere at any given moment in time except *living in* that moment in time.

Lifestyle is learning to *be* wherever you are. It is developing a unique focus on the current moment, and drawing from it all of the substance and wealth of experience and emotions that it has to offer. Lifestyle is taking time to watch a sunset. Lifestyle is listening to silence. Lifestyle is capturing each moment so that it becomes a new part of what we are and of what we are in the process of becoming. Lifestyle is not something we do, it is something we experience. And until we learn to *be* there, we will never master the art of living well.

Letting Life Touch Us

There is a world of difference between *going* to Paris and *experiencing* Paris. Going is a basic physical activity; experiencing is a rich emotional event.

To experience life, we must let it touch us. And not just the positive experiences. We must also be touched by the sorrows and the sadness, by the losses and the longings. Emotions enrich our lives and create for us a special uniqueness in terms of both who we are and how we live.

To live a unique life we must first become unique individuals by experiencing a broad range of human experiences and emotions. Only when we have experienced the full spectrum of human existence can we begin to design and live a life of substance.

All progress begins with an *emotion*. We do not attract a better life merely by *wanting* it, we attract it by adopting the emotions that those with the "better life" possess.

If we want to be happy, we begin by thinking and feeling and acting "happy."

If we want to be wealthy, we begin by thinking and feeling and acting "wealthy."

Any father who wishes to can capture the attention and the appreciation of his family with his *present* resources. He does not have to wait for the wealth in order to discover and share the happiness. He does not have to wait in order to be unique. He does not have to postpone the experience of happiness and a unique lifestyle because it is within his *present* reach. In fact, by practicing what is within his present reach, it will actually *extend* his reach. He only has to start with where he is and with what he has. He needs only to breathe happiness and uniqueness into his assets of the *current* moment.

The joy that could be shared by surprising his daughter with a twenty-dollar concert ticket, when that is all he can currently do, can be just as rewarding as giving her a twenty thousand dollar automobile. This is especially true if, in the past, he has argued with his daughter about her insistence on wanting to "waste money on such foolishness" as a concert. Imagine the father – the head of the family who wants to be sophisticated and wealthy – crumbling up a twenty dollar bill and throwing it at his daughter as an expression of his disapproval about the concert that is so important to her!

How much better it would be if he were to surprise his daughter one day by going out of his way to purchase the ticket for her in advance, and then presenting it to her in some special manner and with a few special words. How much more meaningful still it would be if the father were to purchase *two* tickets and attend the concert *with* his daughter. Perhaps as an added touch he could combine the concert with a private dinner at a special place where the food would be extraordinary and the service unique because of the way the tip was presented.

That is what lifestyle is all about: finding unique ways of transforming emotional possibilities into meaningful experiences that are within our current means.

We can start right *now* by offering all that is within our power to share. Whether we offer our time, a shoulder to cry on, a word of sincere appreciation or our undivided attention, if we will just be there and really live that moment, what an experience that could be!

We must not let the years, and the chances, and the small opportunities for creating moments of joy slip away. If we continue to wait until we have the resources to do the *big* things before we master the art of experiencing all that life currently has to offer, then we may find that we have waited too long.

Let us begin this very day the process of creating a wealth of experiences and memories that will endure in the hearts of those we love long after we are gone.

Lifestyle is a source of joy and fulfillment that is available to us all, regardless of our current circumstances. It is within the immediate reach of anyone who is willing to make it a serious study.

Our lives are filled with opportunities for experiencing a new level of happiness and sophistication and appreciation. All that is required is a change of mind and a decision to begin experiencing it all *now*. And as we demonstrate our new commitment to take full measure from even the smallest opportunities that come our way, life will see to it that far greater experiences than we have ever dreamed of are not long in becoming our certain reward.

DEVELOPING A SENSE OF URGENCY

In summarizing all that we have shared in this book, perhaps it would be accurate to say that our ultimate success or failure depends on three fundamental things:

What we *know*;

How we *feel* about what we know, and;

What we *do* with, and about, all that we feel and all that we know.

But there is another fundamental that must be mastered if we are truly serious about making meaningful changes in our lives. This last fundamental is the glue that holds together all of the pieces to the life puzzle.

You see, it is quite possible that even after applying all of the principles we have discussed in this book, some people will still fall far short of their objectives. Despite all of their efforts to refine their philosophy, to develop an attitude that is conducive to success, to work harder on themselves, to study their results, and to live a more unique lifestyle, all that they dream of becoming, seeing, having and experiencing may still elude them.

Why would those who seem to be serious about making these important changes still be wandering around in circles rather than moving ahead? Why would those who are planting their seeds fail to reap a bountiful harvest?

The Human Comfort Zone

Perhaps part of the answer to these questions may be that it is because we already have so *much* that we tend to settle for so *little*.

Just about everyone has a place to live, a phone, a television, a car, and some source of income. We have clothes to wear and food to eat. With our basic needs taken care of, we drift into a dangerous place called "the comfort zone." We lack either the sense of overwhelming desperation or the incredible force of inspiration to drive us into the marketplace. We might often wish for more. We might frequently want more. But we have neither a burning need nor a burning desire to do what it takes to have more.

The most dangerous aspect of the comfort zone is that it seems to affect our hearing. The more comfortable we are, the more oblivious we become to the sound of the ticking clock. Because there always seems to be so much time ahead of us, we unwittingly squander the present moment. We use it for entertaining ourselves rather than for preparing ourselves.

Those who live in the comfort zone seem to have developed a strange philosophy about human immortality. "I have all of the time I need to carve out my personal success story. There's always tomorrow. There's always next week, next month, next year. There is no real cause for concern. There is no real need to do anything about changing right now. After all, it won't always be the way it is...*by this time next year* things will be different for me."

And so for now – for this moment and for this day – those who are full of good intentions about improving their circumstances remain content with things as they are. Today will be a day for relaxation, or for making more plans, or watching a little TV, or for gathering strength for the new offensive against mediocrity that will begin *tomorrow*.

"Tomorrow I will get up early, and stay up late, and invest all my talent and resources for the purpose of making a dramatic change in my life," says the person with good intentions but no sense of urgency. "I read three books last month, so I think I'll take this month off. I worked hard this week, so I think I'll just relax tomorrow. I should probably make that call today...but what's another day. Tomorrow will do."

Small errors in judgement, repeated every day...

Today Is Yesterday's Tomorrow

The problem with waiting until tomorrow is that when it finally arrives, it is called *today*.

Today is *yesterday's* tomorrow. The question is what did we do with *its* opportunity? All too often we will waste tomorrow as we wasted yesterday, and as we are wasting today. All that could have been accomplished can easily elude us, despite our intentions, until we inevitably discover that the things that *might have been* have slipped from our embrace a single, unused day at a time.

Each of us must pause frequently to remind ourselves that the clock *is* ticking. The same clock that began to tick from the moment we drew our first breath will also someday cease.

Time is the great equalizer of all mankind. It has taken away the best and the worst of us without regard for either.

Time offers opportunity but demands a sense of urgency.

The Two-Minute Warning

It is interesting to watch football teams on a Sunday afternoon. They spend the first fifty-eight minutes routinely following the game plan they *thought* would result in victory. Then something rather remarkable happens. An official walks onto the center of the field and announces what has come to be known as the "Two-Minute Warning."

What happens in the following one hundred and twenty seconds is frequently awesome. We often witness more intensity, more cleverness, more expended energy, and more action compacted into those two final minutes than occurs in the previous fifty-eight.

Why?

A sudden awareness of the sense of imminent defeat, and the birth of a new and sharpened sense of urgency. The participants know that the clock will show no favoritism. The clock will merely do what clocks are supposed to do: They will tick away the seconds until the game is finally over.

The team that finds itself on the threshold of defeat might have shown an extraordinary level of ingenuity and intensity at any time throughout the game. They had the *potential* and the *opportunity* to outscore their opponents *early* in the game. But sometimes, despite their intentions, the players make only an average effort until it is *too* late. Sometimes the blowing of the whistle announcing the two-minute warning is merely a formality signifying the probability of impending and irreversible defeat.

And so it is with the individual human life. The seconds slip into minutes, and the minutes into hours, and the hours into days until we awaken one morning to discover that the moments of opportunity are gone. We spend our

114

final years reliving dreams that might have been, regreting all that never was and now never will be.

When the game of life is finally over, there is no second chance to correct our errors. The clock that is ticking away the moments of our lives does not care about winners and losers. It does not care about who succeeds or who fails. It does not care about excuses, fairness or equality. The only essential issue is how we played the game.

Regardless of a person's current age, there is a sense of urgency that should drive them into action *now* – this very moment. We should be constantly aware of the value of each and every moment of our lives – moments that seem so insignificant that their loss often goes unnoticed.

We still have all the time we need. We still have lots of chances...lots of opportunities...lots of years to show what we can do. For most of us, there *will be* a tomorrow, a next week, a next month, and a next year. But unless we develop a sense of urgency, those brief windows of time will be sadly wasted as were the weeks and months and years before them. There *isn't* an endless supply!

Learn To See A Picture Of The Future In Advance

If we could capture the mental picture in our minds of how the future will be, given our current direction, perhaps we would become more serious about our lives. The following story illustrates dramatically the consequences of failing to develop a sense of urgency.

One day a man was sitting in his small boat on the Niagara River. The waters were calm, the breeze was gentle, and the sun shone brightly from a cloudless sky. Only moments before, the man had pushed his boat from the river bank, and even now the shore was only a few feet away. Clearly, there was no cause for concern. As he baited his hook and cast his line into the water, his mind began to drift.

115

And so did his small boat. The movement was slow and imperceptible in the beginning, with the boat doing what any boat will do when left to drift along with the gentle current. But all drifts are leading toward an eventual destination, and left uncorrected will move toward that destination as though by some strange and unseen force.

In his preoccupations of the moment, the man did not notice the increased movement of his boat. His thoughts were still on fishing as they had been all week in anticipation of this outing. There would be plenty of time for seriousness. For a little while at least, he would continue to relax and enjoy himself. He would ignore the challenges of life and use this hour to allow himself to drift.

Without warning, his thoughts were shaken from wherever they had wandered, back to the present. The sound seemed to come from nowhere, distant at first, but in the twinkling of an eye, it had intensified and was now almost deafening. His attention was seized not only by the sound, but by the movement, for his small boat was being propelled through waters that were no longer gentle and calming.

He looked around him and for the first time he noticed the river banks on either side had retreated as though on a journey of their own. He had no motor on his small boat and had journeyed forth with only a single paddle. There had been no apparent need for a motor or oars.

He struggled to comprehend what was happening, for it was as though he had moved from the calmness, the serenity, and the safety of one environment into the frenzied turbulence of circumstances beyond his ability to grasp or control.

In an instant the reality of his circumstances registered clearly. The thundering sound, the rising foam, the swirling mist, and the uncontrolled momentum of his boat created an instant picture of his horrid circumstances. He had cast himself and his small boat onto the Niagara River, and his drift had brought him to the threshold of the falls.

His mind flashed a collage of thoughts and emotions. If only he had thought about the consequences of his drift. If only he had been better prepared and had thought to equip his boat with a motor, just in case. If only he had noticed sooner, or if only...

Only now did the man notice the crowd that had gathered along the far banks on either side, as the word quickly spread about the boat cascading down the river toward irreversible disaster. It was as though those who knew what was about to happen were wanting to help, but to make any attempt to rescue this hopeless creature would serve only to jeopardize their own safety. Some made futile efforts to toss ropes or to hold out tree branches, but most stood in stunned silence, witnesses to a tragedy that need not have happened.

In a fleeting moment he felt the impending doom of his own personal neglect. He was a victim of his own preoccupation – of his careless inattention to detail in an environment that had the capacity to swallow up his existence, his opportunities and his abilities, and to put all of his dreams to an end in one brief moment.

His one final thought was what he would do differently if only he had a second chance. His thoughts rushed through his mind with the same rapidity as the water passing over the edge of falls, tumbling to their final destination hundreds of feet below.

Had he been given the gift of a second chance he would have allowed himself to see the possible future disaster well in advance. He would have seen it clearly in his mind before the event took place in reality. He would have *anticipated* the certain consequences of neglect. In his mind's eye, he would have seen the rising foam, heard the roar of the falls and sensed his accelerated drift so

117

that he might have acted without delay to move quickly to the safety of the shore.

If he could have been plucked from the waters instead of being consumed by them, he would have placed new value upon his talent, his opportunities and his time. He would not have allowed frivolity to capture his attention nor would he have permitted his desire for rest and relaxation to take his focus off the greater need for intense labor and measurable progress.

But unfortunately, he simply ran out of time.

Examining Our Current Drift

And so it is with our lives. We are all drifting in some direction even at this very moment. The only thing we can determine with any degree of accuracy is where our current drift may be taking us. The big unknown is whether there are still enough ticks left on our personal clocks to change it.

For some people, their past deeds have charted a course which threatens to imprison their future, and yet they do not take corrective and immediate action. They allow the drift of neglect to continue unabated. They permit their desire for entertainment to subdue their appetite for education. Rather than searching, they become lost. They are inclined to think that their small mistakes or neglects or errors in judgement don't really matter all that much. They have not yet learned that everything affects everything else, and that their actions of today are forming their consequences of tomorrow. Their careless acts and their wandering thoughts are swallowing up their most precious resource – *time*. It is because they seemed to have so *much* time that they allowed the individual moments of opportunity to slip unnoticed into an accumulation of empty years.

Our philosophy is moving us toward a specific future

condition. So is our current attitude, level of activity, and results. Our current lifestyle is either encouraging us to experience new depths of emotional experience or whispering to us to wait until we have it all.

What we are and *how* we are must be examined not only in the light of our objectives, but also with a keen awareness of the ticking clock. Maybe we only have a few years left. Maybe we only have a few months left. But wouldn't it make more sense to be doing something constructive with the time that remains than to be passively waiting for time to take its inevitable toll?

Life Is Not A Practice Session

The time for practice is over. Practice time was while we were growing up. Practice time was while we were in school.

We are now full participants in the game of life and our opponent is human mediocrity. In the absence of intense and intelligent human activity, the weeds of failure will move in to destroy the small amount of progress that our efforts have created. We cannot afford to wait for the "two-minute warning." We cannot afford to wait until the last few minutes to discover that our game plan wasn't working. And we cannot afford to wait until the last few ticks of the clock to become intense about life's opportunities.

We must challenge ourselves right now with a new level of thinking, and drive ourselves toward a new level of achievement.

We must impose upon ourselves a new discipline, and develop a new attitude about life that motivates *us* and inspires *others*.

We cannot keep waiting for a foolproof opportunity to come by before we force ourselves to get serious. We must identify our current opportunity and embrace it. We must breathe our talent and our vigor and our new sense of urgency into its existence and discover all that we *can* do.

We cannot allow ourselves to dwell upon the risks in every opportunity. Instead, we must seize the opportunity that is inherent in every risk, knowing that we must sometimes run the risk of going *too far* in order to discover how far we really *can go*.

★ ★ ★

You can do it! You can change your life, and you can start right now simply by developing a new sense of urgency.

Remember, the clock is ticking. You have the ability to achieve whatever you want if you will just begin the process *now*.

It is *easy* to achieve success *and* happiness. And it is easy *not* to achieve them.

The final result of *your* life will be determined by whether you made too many errors in judgement, repeated every day or whether you dedicated your life to a few simple disciplines, *practiced* every day –

The discipline of strengthening and broadening your *philosophy*.

The discipline of developing a better *attitude*.

The discipline of engaging in more intense and consistent *activity* that will lead to the achievement of greater *results*.

The discipline of studying your results in order to anticipate the future more objectively.

The discipline of living life more fully and investing all of your experiences in your better future.

These are the challenges to which you must apply your talent and your intensity with a sense of urgency and unshakeable resolve.

May the pieces to *your* life puzzle come together

smoothly, and may you enjoy the picture of that finished masterpiece as a result of your unwaivering commitment to mastering the basics.

Let your efforts and results give cause to those who will one day gather to pass judgement on your existence to speak only the simple phrase...

Well done, good and faithful servant.

Over 200 titles available including all Jim Rohn Books, CDs, DVDs and Training Programs, plus:

CD/VIDEO/DVD

The Psychology of Winning – Denis Waitley (6 CDs)
Secrets of Closing the Sale – Zig Ziglar (12 CDs)
The Psychology of Selling – Brian Tracy (6 CDs)
Raising Positive Kids in a Negative World – Zig Ziglar (6 CDs)
The Art of Exceptional Living – Jim Rohn (6 CDs)
Choosing Your Future – Les Brown (6 CDs)
Memory in a Month – Ron White (6 CDs)

TRAINING PACKAGES

The Platinum Collection – Denis Waitley (18 CDs)
Success Mastery Academy – Brian Tracy (16 CDs/wb)
2004 Jim Rohn Weekend Event (12 DVDs, 24 CDs plus 283-page workbook)
The Complete How to Stay Motivated Package – Zig Ziglar (3 Volumes plus Performance Planner)

and Many More...

Order by mail, phone or fax.
Payment: Check, Mastercard, VISA, AmEx or Discover

SHIPPING & HANDLING

For Orders	Please Add
Up to $24.99	$4.95
$25 to $74.99	$5.95
$75 to $149.99	$6.95
$150 to $299.99	$8.95
$300 and Over	**3%**

Applies to US orders sent UPS Ground.
Call for quotes on International and overnight shipping.

Mix and Match Pricing on Denis Waitley, Zig Ziglar, Jim Rohn and Brian Tracy Excerpt Booklets

	Regular	20% OFF
1	$1.50 each	$1.30 each
2-9	$1.25 each	$1.00 each
10-24	$1.00 each	$ .80 each
25-99	$ .90 each	$ .72 each
100-599	$ .80 each	$ .64 each
600-1199	$ .65 each	$ .52 each
1200+	$ .60 each	$ .48 each

All prices are in U.S. Dollars

JIM ROHN

ONE OF AMERICA'S MOST
SOUGHT-AFTER SUCCESS COUNSELORS

For more than 39 years, Jim Rohn has focused on the fundamentals of human behavior that most affect personal and business performance. Jim is the standard to which those who seek to teach and inspire others are compared. He possesses the unique ability to bring extraordinary insights to ordinary principles and events, and the combination of his substance and style captures the imagination of those who hear or read his words.

Jim Rohn has been hailed over the years as one of the most influential thinkers of our time and has helped motivate and train an entire generation of personal development trainers as well as hundreds of executives from America's top corporations.

Jim Rohn has now shared his message with over 6,000 audiences and over 4 million people. He has conducted his seminars and workshops throughout Europe, Asia, Australia, and Africa, as well as in most principle cities in North America. He is a member of the National Speakers Association and a recipient of its coveted CPAE award, given to him in 1985 for outstanding performance and professionalism in speaking.

I wish for you a life of wealth, health, and happiness; a life in which you give to yourself the gift of patience, the virtue of reason, the value of knowledge, and the influence of faith in your own ability to dream about and to achieve worthy reward.

Jim Rohn